WOODWARD'S
VICTORIAN ARCHITECTURE
AND RURAL ART

A facsimile of volume one (1867) and
volume two (1868)

AMERICAN LIFE FOUNDATION

Library of Victorian Culture

1978

ISBN: 0-89257-044-X

THIS BOOK RE-UNITES two rare architectural stylebooks first published in 1867 and 1868 by one of Victorian America's most prolific architectural book publishers — George Everston Woodward.

A passage from the introduction to volume two best sums up the function of these books: "In No 1. of this series a large number of designs were given for low-priced cottages, farm houses, etc., together with numerous plans for barns and all classes of out-buildings, and designs for laying out and embellishing small plots up to ten acres in extent. This number [i.e., No. 2] is devoted more particularly to a class of houses comtemplating a more liberal expenditure, and introducing examples of the French or Mansard roof, which is attracting attention from all; and when amount of room is considered, is as economical as any style that can be selected."

In volume one, Woodward said he was "indebted for assistance in preparing the designs to E. C. Hussey," an architect having an office in the same building as Woodward — 191 Broadway. In 1874 Woodward published Hussey's *National Cottage Architecture,* but Hussey is best known for *Home Building* (1875) — a book which The American Life Foundation re-published in The Library of Victorian Culture in 1975.

Other designers represented in volume one were: G. E. Harney of Cold Springs, NY for building designs 18, 21, 31, 39, and 57; E. Ferrand of Detroit, MI for landscape designs 13, 17, 36, and 56; and E. A. Bauman of Rahway, NJ for 19 and 58.

In volume two: G. E. Harney did designs 1, 3, 5, 8, and 10; Robert Mook of New York City did number 4; Carl Pfeiffer of New York City did numbers 7 and 12; and F. S. Copley, a Tompkinsville, NY artist, did number 9.

This book is the companion volume to *Woodward's Country Homes* (1865) which The American Life Foundation re-published in The Library of Victorian Culture in 1977.

WOODWARD'S

ARCHITECTURE

AND RURAL ART.

No. I.——1867.

BY

GEO. E. WOODWARD,

ARCHITECT AND CIVIL ENGINEER,

AUTHOR OF " WOODWARD'S COUNTRY HOMES."

NEW YORK:

GEO. E. WOODWARD, 191 BROADWAY.

CONTENTS.

vi CONTENTS.

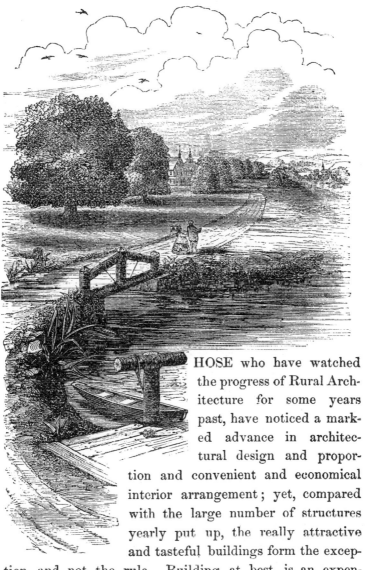

HOSE who have watched
the progress of Rural Architecture for some years
past, have noticed a marked advance in architec-
tural design and propor-
tion and convenient and economical
interior arrangement; yet, compared
with the large number of structures
yearly put up, the really attractive
and tasteful buildings form the excep-
tion, and not the rule. Building, at best, is an expensive undertaking, and those who engage in it without

availing themselves of the progressive improvements of the day, make investments from which it is difficult to realize first cost; while he who embraces the principles of beauty, harmony, good taste, etc., rarely fails to command his customer, and a handsome profit when ready to sell. The fact we desire to impress most thoroughly is, that it costs no more to build correctly and beautifully than to ignore all rules of taste, and that every one in this broad land who means to have a home of his own, should have a home worth owning.

The designs shown are mostly of a low-priced description, and the prevailing style chosen is the rural Gothic, the best that is known for cottage structures, being the most economical and useful. Nearly all the designs admit of shingle roofs, which places the workmanship under the owner's control. In new countries, slate and tin roofers, and their materials, are not always available. Handy farm-laborers can shave shingles and make their own roofs; and the pioneer, the well-to-do farmer, the laborer, and the mechanic usually expect to aid in erecting their own buildings.

It is proposed, however, to introduce all the varied styles of architecture in future numbers, and they may be looked for with interest as supplying from year to year the latest and best models in the progress of Rural Art.

A moderate number of plans for laying out small tracts of land are given; and as our descriptions must necessarily be brief, the illustrations have been so managed as to tell their own story. Many designs for necessary outbuildings are introduced, as the plan of this book covers all departments of Rural Art. No pains or expense have been spared in making this work reliable. All designs are of a practical character, can be enlarged and worked from; many of them are from actual construction, and all are worth study and attention from any one who contemplates building. We mean that it shall supply a want long felt for designs for convenient and attractive homes for the million. We are largely indebted for assistance in preparing the designs to Mr. E. C. Hussey. Most of the engravings are by Mr. Chas. Spiegle, both of whom have executed their work in a thoroughly artistic and satisfactory manner

FIG. 2.—DESIGN FOR AN ICE-HOUSE.

Fig. 3.—Cottage.

  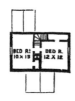

Fig. 4.—Cellar Plan.   Fig. 5.—First Floor.   Fig. 6.—Second Floor.

DESIGN No. 2.

A LOW-PRICED COTTAGE.

This design of two rooms on each floor gives a good deal of available space with independent entrances to each room. To those who must have houses at the lowest possible sum, the bay-window, porch, and finials may be omitted at first, and added at a future day; but by all means preserve the broad projecting roof and the general outline as shown. Let the first-floor ceiling be 8 feet, and use studding of the usual length of 13 feet; this will give a breast of about 3½ feet in second story. Make the height in center 8 feet, and the roof about one third to one half pitch; that is, the height of the roof should be one third or one half the width of the building. Additions can be made at any time when wanted, and will rather add to than detract from the general appearance. The cost of this cottage will range all the way from $600 to $1,200; and this difference exists in nearly all classes of buildings, according to the section of country in which they are built, the facility of getting materials, and the business management of the owner. As prices are constantly changing, it is useless to make statements that are only calculated to mislead; indeed, at no former period could prices be furnished without creating much mischief. The best way is to show the nearest good mechanic the design, tell him, as near as possible, your wishes, and he can give the most reliable figures.

FIG. 7.—A COMPACT COTTAGE.

FIG. 8.—CELLAR PLAN.   FIG. 9.—FIRST FLOOR.   FIG. 10.—SECOND FLOOR.

DESIGN No. 3.

A COMPACT COTTAGE.

WE show here a design for a very pretty, compact cottage, that may be erected either with wood, stone, or brick. Rock-faced rubble masonry, over which vines may be trained, would, we think, be very suitable. Those who build houses like this can easily find purchasers for them; indeed, acre-lots in the suburbs of our cities and larger villages, with tasty cottages and a moderate amount of landscape embellishment, would not remain uncalled-for many days. There is a certain steady demand for cosy, comfortable homes adapted to the purses of the great masses that should attract more attention from capitalists. Any convenient locality, where the nucleus, composed of a store, a church, a school-house, and a first-rate hotel, can be established, could be made very attractive, and induce many to leave the crowded and unhealthy tenements of the city for a home in the country, be it ever so small. The complete cost of such an establishment in the country, at a less distance in point of time from the City Hall of New York city than Thirty-fifth Street, would not exceed the yearly rental of a not much more commodious house in the city, while its annual increasing value amounts to more than the legal rate of interest.

FIG. 11.—AN OCTAGONAL COTTAGE.

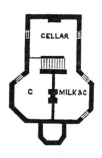
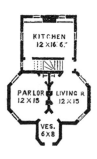
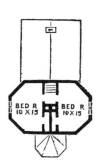

FIG. 12.--CELLAR PLAN   FIG. 13.—FIRST FLOOR.   FIG. 14.—SECOND FLOOR.

DESIGN No. 4.

AN OCTAGONAL COTTAGE.

FOR the sake of a little variety in form, we here introduce a cottage having octagonal ends, and the principal rooms on the first floor of octagonal form. These rooms, furnished with a fair degree of taste, will present a cosy appearance. The roof covers the building in the same manner as if it had square corners, and is supported by a neat bracket of timber-work. Those who do not fancy this suggestion, can adopt a similar plan with square angles at the corners, and omit the brackets under the roof. The arrangement of the windows in the octagon ends gives better facilities for ventilation than if both windows were on the same line of wall, which they would have to be to preserve the symmetry of a square room. In the construction of this house use the "balloon frame," because it is stronger and forty per cent. cheaper than any other—for a full illustrated description of which see "Woodward's Country Homes." Instead of filling in with brick, sheath the outside of the studding horizontally with rough boards, and over this put the siding; a layer of tarred paper placed between would be serviceable. This will make a strong, warm house.

FIG. 15.—A FARM-COTTAGE.

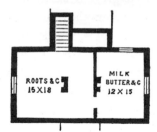

FIG. 16.—CELLAR PLAN.

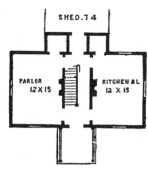

FIG. 17.—FIRST FLOOR.

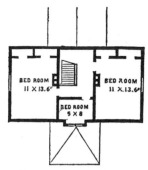

FIG. 18.—SECOND FLOOR.

DESIGN No. 5.

A FARM COTTAGE.

THIS design will answer well for a farm-cottage, presents a good variety, and would be considered an attractive home. We have had in view a moderate expenditure, and of course the builder must be satisfied with a moderate amount of room. Prices we might give, if we were satisfied they would be any guide; but a book like this, having a national circulation, can not be of any value whatever as to cost of construction. We have seen the time when, in the immediate vicinity of New York, this cottage could be built for $500, or even less. It might possibly be built now for $1,200; yet in some sections of the country, labor and materials can be had for half the prices they command here. There are many portions of the West where, at the present time (fall of 1866), this cottage could be fully completed for $400 to $500. An ingenious farmer, who can supply from his farm a considerable portion of the materials, do his own hauling, and with the aid of a skillful mechanic and one or two handy laborers, if the work be not pushed on too fast, could execute this and similar designs by the use of very little money.

FIG. 19.—ICE-HOUSE.

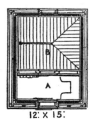

12: × 15:

FIG. 20.—PLAN OF FIG. 19.

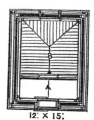

12: × 15:

FIG. 21.—PLAN OF FIG. 22

FIG. 22.—ICE-HOUSE.

DESIGNS Nos. 6 AND 7.

ICE-HOUSES.

ICE is an article that may, with many, be considered indispensable. Those who have enjoyed its use are unwilling to do without it. The comforts of the household are materially increased, and an abundant supply is a great luxury.

Ice-houses may be constructed to suit all tastes and purses; and the various designs we give can be built plainly as well as elaborately. About twelve feet cube of ice is the requisite quantity for most families, and a bulk of this size keeps better than if smaller. The best houses are those built entirely above ground, though one, as shown in fig. 19, which is built into a gravelly bank is not objectionable. Thorough drainage is essential, and where a pipe is used, it should be trapped, to prevent a current of air. The sides should be double, with from 8 to 12 inches space, and packed with wet tan, sawdust, or pulverized charcoal, well rammed down. Sometimes double walls of this kind are made, with an air chamber between; and sometimes an air chamber is made by furring out and lining with boards only. At the bottom we prefer, after the drainage has been provided, to lay a good plank floor; cover this with 6 or 8 inches of sawdust or tan, and then pack the ice (which should be from 6 to 8 inches or more in thickness) in layers, putting the blocks as close together as possible, and chinking up with small pieces of ice or snow. A space of about 6 inches should be left between the mass of ice and the sides of the house, which should be thoroughly packed with sawdust or tan. When the house is full, put over all the ice a layer of sawdust or tan at least one foot in thickness, and pack it down thoroughly. A good roof should be provided, and ventilation of a most thorough character. A draft of air through the ice would soon destroy it; a draft of air above it only is an essential preservative. In constructing these houses, it would be better, in addition to the openings shown, to leave a space from six inches to one foot wide, under the eaves, above the plate, both sides the entire length of the house. This opening is protected from the rain, and the free admission of air thus secured is of great advantage.

Straw and hay are used sometimes for packing in place of sawdust or tan, but are not so serviceable. In each of these designs there is a cooling-room attached for milk, butter, meats, fruits, etc., marked A on the plans. The room marked B is the one in which the ice is packed; the floor is laid so that the drainage runs to one point, and is carried off by a pipe trapped, to prevent the admission of air.

ORNAMENTS IN LANDSCAPE GARDENING.

DESIGN No. 8.

FIG. 23.—RUSTIC STAND.

WILD ground and irregular surfaces call for rude and bold work. Here introduce rustic bridges crossing ravines, rustic seats, vases, baskets of rustic work, gnarled and curious roots encircling boxes of plants, hollow stumps and dead trees supporting climbing plants, rustic kiosks on spots which offer agreeable resting-places and command fine views; all such objects are appropriate to grounds so characterized.   There is no particular beauty in a piece of rustic work in itself, but when properly placed it becomes beautiful from its association, and in turn enhances the picturesque of the grounds about.

DESIGN No. 9.

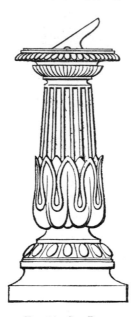

FIG. 24.—SUN-DIAL.

AMONG the many objects used for adornment, there is a very pretty one which we would like to see more frequently employed, and which when properly placed by the side of some walk well retired from other objects, is

in itself highly suggestive. We refer to the *Sun-dial.*
What thoughts this monitor suggests to the mind! how
silent, yet how eloquent! His must be a vacant mind indeed who can pass such a teacher without finding thought
to accompany his walk. A shadow teacheth us, and we
learn in the end that we have pursued but shadows.

In the beautiful words of the poet:

> "This shadow on the dial's face,
>   That steals from day to day,
>   With slow, unseen, unceasing pace,
>   Moments, and months, and years away;
>   This shadow, which in every clime,
>   Since light and motion first began,
>   Hath held its course sublime—
>   What is it? Mortal man!
>   It is the scythe of time—
>   A shadow only to the eye;
>   Yet in its calm career
>   It levels all beneath the sky;
>   And still, through each succeeding year
>   Right onward with resistless power,
>   Its stroke shall darken every hour,
>   Till nature's race be run,
>   And time's last shadow shall eclipse the sun."

FIG. 25.—WELL-HOUSE.

Fig. 26.—Perspective.

Fig. 27.—Cellar Plan.

Fig. 28.—First Floor.

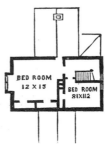

Fig. 29.—Second Floor.

DESIGN No. 10.

THE additions of porches, verandas, bay-windows, etc., increase the effect of cottage-houses to a very considerable degree, add much to interior convenience and beauty, and, if put on at the time when the building is constructed, do not materially augment the expense. We think they are always worth their full cost, and rarely fail to make an impression upon the eye of a purchaser. The interior wood-work of this cottage, or any other, should be selected with some little care, and all stained —either satin-wood or light black-walnut. These stains, which can be easily procured, are better if laid on in oil, and then, if covered with two coats of varnish, make the nearest approach possible to the appearance of the above-named natural woods. No grainer's art can do as well. Handsomely stained and varnished wood-work is, we think, the most superior mode of treating interiors. It adds much to the warmth and cosiness of the rooms, has the effect of furnishing, and, so far as cleanliness is concerned, is of great help to the housekeeper. This style of finish, whether for the humble cottage or costly mansion, is better and more attractive, if done with good taste, than the most costly and elaborately painted tints.

FIG. 30.

FIG. 31 —CELLAR PLAN.

FIG. 32.—FIRST FLOOR.

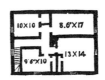

FIG. 33.—SECOND FLOOR.

DESIGN No. 11.

THIS design can, for the amount of room afforded, be constructed very cheaply. The kitchen is shown in the basement plan, but can be put on the first floor, or in a rear addition, if deemed more convenient. If built in an exposed situation, some filling-in between the studding will be necessary. There are several modes of doing this, all of which add to the stiffness and solidity of the frame, and ward off the searching winds. An air chamber for confined or dead air adds much to winter warmth and summer coolness, and this is usually provided for. The most common mode of filling-in is with soft brick laid on edge in mortar; grout is also made use of. Back plastering, or lathing between studs—nailing common laths or rough pieces against strips fastened to each side of the studs and covered with coarse mortar—is serviceable. Where lumber is plenty, cover the frame with rough boards, and put the weather-boarding on the outside of the rough boarding; this we have found answers an excellent purpose. A layer of common tarred roofing-paper between the two courses of boarding will render the house impenetrable to wind or rain, and affords one of the best means of protection.

DESIGN No. 12.

A HOUSE FOR DRYING FRUITS.

THE following sketch, received from J. C. Hobson, Esq., Cardington, Ohio, is of a building of moderate dimensions, 4 by 12 feet, and 5 feet in height, set upon a wall of brick or stone 20 inches high; and to obviate the necessity of going inside when heated up for drying, it is constructed with two tiers of drawers on either side, 23 inches by 5 feet, with slat or wire bottoms, each one made to slide in and out independent of the rest, and each tier inclosed with double doors. The building is heated by means of furnaces extending from either end, and communicating with the flue in the center.

FIG. 34.—DRYING-HOUSE.

By reason of the drawers meeting over the furnaces in the middle, the heat in rising is compelled to pass through them, thus the fruit is dried faster than by the usual mode of placing it on shelves against the wall of the house.

The number of drawers may be increased to double the amount represented in the drawing, if necessary, which would make them hold a considerable quantity of fruit, say from twenty to thirty bushels.

DESIGN No. 13.

PLAN FOR LAYING OUT A SQUARE ACRE LOT.

BY E FERRAND, DETROIT, MICH.

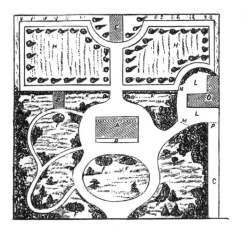

FIG. 35.

A, Dwelling.
B, Piazza.
C, Passage from the Barn to the Street.
D, Greenhouse.
E, Grapery (house).
F, Flower-beds.
H, Kitchen Garden, with dwarf fruit-trees and small fruits.
K, Trellis of grapevines.
L, Yard.
M, Gate.
N, Gate.
O, Stable, Barn, and other Out-buildings.

ORNAMENTAL ROADS.

A PROPER location of an ornamental road adds to it, we may say, all of its character and importance, and it may be made in inexperienced hands a very tame and meaningless affair. To locate and make a road that shall fulfill only a useful purpose is one thing; to so locate it that it shall comply with all the requisites sought for in ornamental grounds, is quite another matter. Whatever there is of consequence should be made the most of, and by the most graceful and easy lines of curvature should destroy the thought that anything of the kind was intended. The entrance, the perspective view of the dwelling, the easy grade, the drainage, construction, planting, etc., are only thoroughly considered by those of extensive practice.

Where proper materials for road metal can not be had, or where expense is to be avoided, the earth road must be adopted. To make this is an easy matter; thorough drainage, wherever necessary, should be most carefully done. The bed of the road should have a crowning of about 4 inches in a width of 16 feet, or half an inch to a foot, both ways from sides, as shown in fig. 36. The sods at the edge should be kept low—not over $1\frac{1}{2}$ inches high, except in such cases as where surface drainage crosses the road, and is liable to wash earth on to the lawn. The grade line in the direction of the road should be kept as regular as possible, and avoid undulating. On the surface of the

FIG. 36.—SECTION OF EARTH ROAD.

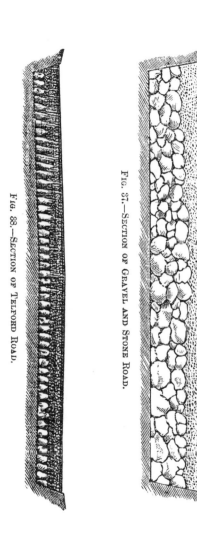

FIG. 37.—SECTION OF GRAVEL AND STONE ROAD.

FIG. 38.—SECTION OF TELFORD ROAD.

road, gravel, coal ashes, oyster shells, or similar materials, may be placed to good advantage, and will make good roads through all the dry seasons. The making of an earth road similar to this is in all cases necessary where the road bed is to be stoned, except that it is taken out to a greater depth. The most common mode of making a stone road is after the manner shown in fig. 37. Stones of unequal size are laid in, or usually thrown in, to a depth varying according to the builder's notion, generally one foot and over, and covered with 4 to 6 inches of gravel. The chief objection to it is, that it requires a larger amount of excavation; if the stones are not carefully hand-packed and rolled, they are liable to work out on the surface; heavy loads, as coal, hay, manure, etc., will cut them up, and weeds will grow thickly and rapidly. In a park, on properly constructed roads in constant use by light carriages, these objections would have no weight. Still, by a greater expenditure of labor in keeping them in order, such roads, when well made, answer a very good purpose; but as an investment they are not so good as other kinds that do not require so much care. The first cost is less than broken stone roads. They should not, under ordinary circumstances, exceed 10 inches of thickness of stone and gravel.

Fig. 38 illustrates the manner of constructing the Telford road, a valuable and well-tested plan, good in all localities where stone can be had, and admits of a softer and inferior quality of stone being used in the pavement. Telford approved of a level cross grade instead of a convex surface. Hughes, a later author, declares the convex

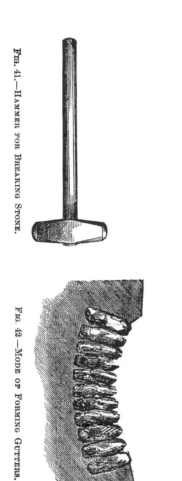

FIG. 41.—HAMMER FOR BREAKING STONE.

FIG. 42.—MODE OF FORMING GUTTERS.

FIG. 40.—SECTION OF BAILDON ROAD.

FIG. 39.—SECTION OF MCADAM ROAD.

line to be the best, which it undoubtedly is. This road is made by first setting a rough pavement of stone, as shown in fig. 37. The projections of the upper part are broken off with a hammer, and the interstices are packed with stone chips or spawls. On this pavement are placed two layers of road metal, and the whole is covered with gravel or some other good binding material. The whole thickness for an ornamental road need not be over 10 to 12 inches.

Fig. 39 shows the manner of making the McAdam road. This consists entirely of road metal; that is, stone broken to a cubical form of 2½ inches, and put on in three layers, each of which is worked together by carriage wheels, and the final surface made smooth by constant use. It becomes in time a solid, compact, impenetrable body, the stone uniting by its own angles, aided by the dust ground from them by constant use. This class of road-making is not adapted for private estates, in consequence of the time and use required to make the surface smooth; and the fine dust is objectionable.

Fig. 40 is a cross section of what is known as the Bayldon system, and is, we think, the most superior manner known of constructing either public highways or private ornamental roads. It consists of a layer of road metal 6 inches in thickness placed on in one solid body, thoroughly rolled, and covered with about 1½ inches of blending material, good gravel being the best. We have, however, in an extensive practice, built these roads with a layer of road metal of 4 to 5 inches thick, and with just gravel enough to finish the surface even, one of which, after eight years of constant use, does not appear to have failed in the slightest particular. It has, through all seasons, presented a hard, smooth, handsome surface. This system of road-making requires the least quantity of excavation, and can be made ready for use at once. Its construction is the simplest of all modes, and its durability and efficiency have stood the test of thirty years.

The prevailing impression is, that the stone and gravel road, fig. 37, is the cheapest to construct; a very doubtful matter, we think, compared with the Bayldon plan. One thing is certain, however, that to keep the stone and gravel road in polished order, in private estates, requires at least four times the care; and if a little is saved in first cost, it is soon balanced by additional expense. Where economy in building a good road is to be considered, the stone might be broken at leisure intervals through the winter, and by those unfitted by age or misfortune from doing the work of able-bodied men. The stone is broken with a steel hammer weighing about 1¾ lbs. (see fig. 41). The stone-breaker sits at his work, and soon becomes very expert. Some use long-handled hammers, and stand up, but can not accomplish much.

Where it becomes necessary to form gutters, we think it best to do so with quarried or fractured stone put together in the usual manner of making a pavement (see fig. 42). The advantage is, that the gravel may be raked in a thin layer on the gutter (which is always unsightly), and the ragged edges of the stone will hold it, and prevent its being washed. Cobble-stone gutters answer a good purpose, but can not be so easily concealed.

FIG. 43.—A FARM-HOUSE.

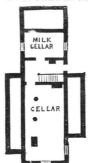

FIG. 44.—CELLAR PLAN.

FIG. 45.—FIRST FLOOR.

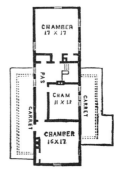

FIG. 46.—SECOND FLOOR.

DESIGN No. 14.

A FARM-HOUSE.

This design is for a farm-house of an irregular exterior form, covered by a roof without valleys, except those by the dormer window.

As the plan provides for sleeping-rooms on the first floor, about the healthiness of which opinions differ, we quote the following from the New York *Tribune* reports of the discussions of the New York Farmers' Club:

" *Sleeping-Rooms, are Elevated Ones most Healthy ?* —Isaac Bond, Washington City.—'Are low-story rooms equally healthy as lodging rooms with those of upper stories ? I have long been led, perhaps more by prejudice, or the opinions of others, than by facts or good reasons, to believe up-stairs decidedly the better; but finding the one-story plans given in Miss Beecher's book, without a hint or misgiving as to their being less healthful, while the sole or chief object of the work, which appears excellent in all other respects, so far as I have read it, is to improve the health of American women, I have been led to question my old opinions, and to inquire whether sleeping on the first floor would do more harm to my whole family of five, than going to the second story about ten times a day would do my wife, who is not very strong, and two very young daughters ? If you can furnish facts or sound reasons bearing upon this question, they will

DESIGN No. 15.

A SOUTHERN HOUSE.

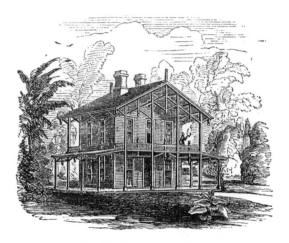

FIG. 47.—PERSPECTIVE VIEW.

FIG. 48.—FIRST FLOOR.

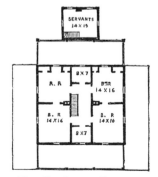

FIG. 49.—SECOND FLOOR.

doubtless benefit many others no less than myself. I may add that economy in building is a very important consideration with me, and I am fully aware that a second story is the cheapest way of getting the same amount of additional room to what we must have in the first story, two rooms, besides wood-shed, etc., as you advise in a late number of the *Tribune.* My situation is on one acre, three miles N.N.W. of the Post-office Department.'

"SOLON ROBINSON—Let us look at a few simple facts, which may, perhaps, upset the writer's prejudice about the unhealthiness of lodging in lower rooms. Nearly all of the ancient farm-houses of New England had one, and frequently three or four beds upon the lower floor. The people in those days certainly were no more unhealthy than they were after it became fashionable to build two or three story houses. About the cruelest wrong of all that a man of ample grounds can inflict upon his family is to build a house which compels them often to traverse long flights of stairs. I am well satisfied, from personal experience and observation, that a properly constructed one-story house upon a dry soil is just as healthy for lodgings upon its lower floor as a higher house would be upon its upper ones. Mr. Bond speaks of the economy of space gained in making two-story houses instead of one. Should the health, comfort, and life of the occupants be sacrificed to economy? Besides, it is only economy in the first cost of building material; in all after-years it is a serious loss of labor to all the family who are compelled to ascend to an upper story daily, and frequently hourly, to perform their necessary household duties. An up-stairs sick-room

DESIGN No. 16.

A COTTAGE STABLE.

Fig. 50.—Perspective View.

Fig. 51.—Plan.

is particularly inconvenient. It is bad enough for people who live in cities to suffer from such disadvantages. It is positively wicked for a man building in the country to ape the fashion of city houses. Be assured, sir, there is no reason why the lower rooms of a one-story country house should be unhealthy for lodging. Probably one of the main reasons why houses have of late years been built so high is owing to the expensiveness of roofing materials. That difficulty is likely now to be obviated. Roofing made cheap, durable, and safe from danger of fire will tend to a great improvement in the style of our farm-houses. If we discuss the subject enough to awaken the public mind to a sense of its importance, we shall one of these days get back to the comforts of one-story houses.

"R. H. WILLIAMS—I entirely agree with the opinions expressed by Mr. Robinson. I would never recommend building a farm-house over one and a half story high. That is the most economical, as that form will afford all the sleeping-rooms necessary to be placed on the upper floor, at a much less cost than they could be made in a full-storied house, and, besides, it looks more fitting as a farm-house. A two or three story house is inconsistent with the wants of the farm, and shows bad judgment in those who build them. This is one of the most important questions we have had before the Club, and one which affords room for ample discussion. It is sometimes very remarkable to see how one man gives fashion and form to all the dwellings in the vicinity. If some pretentious builder leads off with a high-storied house, no matter how inconvenient, others are very apt to ape the fashion. In one section of this State, the almost universal style is a two-story center, with two one-story wings. The most that can be said of that form is, that it is fashionable. Anything that we can say here to improve the style of farm-houses will be beneficial to a great many people.

"Mr. DISTURNELL contested against lower-floor lodging-rooms, because he was satisfied they were much more unhealthy than upper ones. He endeavored to prove it from some statistics drawn from Cairo, Egypt.

"Mr. ROBINSON said his position was taken for a dry, hard, rocky soil, like that of New England generally, and not for malarious Egypt.

"The CHAIRMAN said that Judge Butler, formerly a physician at Norwalk, Conn., declares that when people were in the habit of sleeping in lower rooms, maladies prevailed which are now seldom heard of, such as a low grade of fevers. He says prevailing fogs never rise above fourteen feet high, and those sleeping in upper rooms escape its influence. His recommendation to all who build country houses is to make the cellar under the entire house, cementing the bottom and sides so thoroughly that no gas can arise from the earth; and never to sleep on the lower floor. Besides keeping the cellar clean, care should also be taken to clean the well every year. Dr. Ward, who lives near the great salt-marshes of New Jersey, says, from his house, which is situated on a hill, he can look down upon the banks of fog lying upon a lower level. All of our sleeping-rooms are upon the upper floors, and, I think, in a more healthy stratum of the atmosphere than they would be if less elevated.

"Dr. Snodgrass—This may be so in that locality, but there are others where the case is reversed. Those living immediately upon the banks of the Potomac, and other Southern rivers, have often escaped malarious diseases, while the houses situated upon the adjoining hills or bluffs were so sickly some seasons as scarcely to be habitable.

" Henry Ward Beecher—A few miles south of Indianapolis, upon a high bluff of White River, one of the highest in that locality, in the early settlement of the country, there was a town built. Upon the opposite side of the river there was a small settlement, but slightly elevated, upon the water level. According to the usual theory about malaria, these houses should have been sickly, and those in the town healthy; the reverse was the fact to such a degree that the town was entirely abandoned, and the houses left to decay and waste. The laws of health are not always to be measured by high or low situations, nor by high or low sleeping-rooms, if they are properly ventilated."

Fig. 52.—A Bird-House.

DESIGN No. 17.

PLAN FOR LAYING OUT A THREE-ACRE LOT.

BY E FERRAND, DETROIT, MICH.

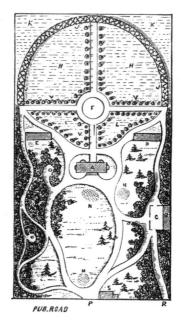

FIG. 53.

A, Dwelling-House.

B, Stable, Barn, etc.

C, Barn-yard, with three openings.

D, Grapery.

E, Greenhouse.

F, Water.

H, Kitchen Garden.

I, Grapevine Arbor.

K, Place for small fruits.

L, Strawberries.

N, Flower-beds.

O, Places for rustic seats

P, Principal E trance.

R, Entrance to the Barn.

S, Gardener's House.

V, Dwarf fruit trees.

THIS garden has the appearance of a much larger place than it really is; in fact, the plan could be applied to a place of ten or more acres just as well as to the limited space of three. The roads are numerous. It is intended for a lot in the proximate vicinity of the city, and to be occupied by a man who has means to keep it in order.

All these gardens are intended for the same purpose, and laid out according to the same principle; that is to say, the most is done to conceal their narrow limits, and leave one to guess how far one may be from the end of it when one is no more than ten feet from the well-concealed fence; at the same time, all the secondary buildings, such as barns, stables, etc., are very close to the main house, though they are entirely out of sight.

In the plan, smoothly-curved walks are drawn in the thickets of large trees; there is also a vine arbor, which is a handsome ornament. The kitchen garden occupies about one acre and a quarter, and is in proportion to the whole extent of the place.

FIG. 54.—CHICKEN-COOP.

FIG. 55.—A SMALL STABLE.

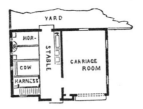

FIG. 56.—GROUND PLAN.

DESIGN No. 18.

A SMALL STABLE.

BY G. E. HARNEY, ARCHITECT, COLD SPRING, PUTNAM CO., N. Y.

THIS design for a small stable has accommodation for two horses and a cow, besides a separate apartment for carriages, and another smaller room for harnesses, etc.

The carriage-room measures 13 feet by 22. Each horse-stall is 5½ feet wide, and 9½ feet long to the rear of the stall partition, or 17 feet to the partition of the carriage-room.

The stalls are provided with cast-iron mangers and iron hay-racks, each secured to opposite corners of the stall. We consider these iron fixtures the best in use, but care should be taken to keep them always coated with some kind of paint, to prevent injury to the horses' mouths in winter, when they are liable to become frosted.

The cow-stall is 4½ feet wide, and is provided with a manger and some suitable fastening apparatus; for the latter, we prefer the ring and chain, though the old-fashioned stanchion is recommended by many.

The floors of the stalls should be laid with smoothly-planed locust joists, slanted toward the gutter just enough to take away the water—say 2 inches in the 9½ feet.

The harness-room is provided with hooks for harness; a closet to keep brushes, soap, oils, medicines, etc., etc., and a small stove to heat water for washing harness, etc.

There is a rain-water cistern, built with brick and cement, in the yard, near the rear of the stable, and this, taking water from the roof, by means of tin conductors, supplies all the water required.

Rain water is much better for stock than spring water. The pump is inside the stable, as will be seen in the plan, and empties into a trough, convenient to which are chests lined with tin, for holding oats and meal, etc.

A ventilating shaft rises from the stable-room to the ventilator shown in the sketch, and this, with the small windows in the head of each stall, provides sufficient circulation of air. In the summer, the doors may be taken off their hinges, and gates with locks substituted in their place. The little windows spoken of are placed *above* the heads of the horses—say 7 feet from the floor, and are opened by means of a pulley and rope.

At the rear of the building, a door opens into a yard inclosed by a high fence ; and if there be a desire to make the establishment quite complete, there may be built around this yard a range of buildings for poultry, pigs, etc., and open sheds for wagons and carts.

This stable is built of wood, and covered with vertical boarding and battens ; the roof is covered with slate ; the doors all have simple hoods as well as the windows; and the glass for the latter we would have set in diamond-shaped panes, which, at a little or no extra expense, heightens wonderfully the artistic effect of such a building as this.

Paint the building a warm cream-color, the eaves, and window-trimmings, and doors considerably darker.

DESIGN No. 19.

PLANS FOR IMPROVEMENT OF GROUNDS.

BY E. A. BAUMANN, RAHWAY, N. J.

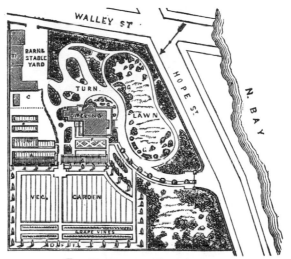

FIG. 57.—PLAN OF FOUR ACRES.

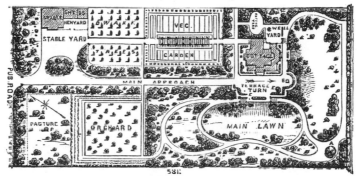

FIG. 58.—PLAN OF FIVE ACRES.

FIG. 59.—PERSPECTIVE VIEW.

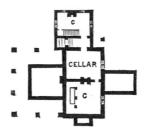

FIG. 60.—CELLAR PLAN.

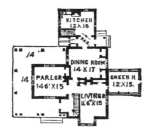

FIG. 61.—FIRST FLOOR.

FIG. 62.—SECOND FLOOR.

DESIGN No. 20.

WE show here a compact, convenient cottage, having a conservatory attached for those who love to gratify their taste for flowers. Each room has a cross draft, and can be abundantly ventilated in warm weather. A passage between the kitchen and dining-room cuts off the smell of cooking, and the doors from the kitchen are double, with spring-hinges, and without locks or other fastenings; they are opened with the foot, and close immediately after passing. The servant can pass in the kitchen through one door and out through the other with a large tray of dishes, and thus avoid meeting any one, while flies and the aroma of cooking have little chance of getting into the main part of the house. We think during the summer months it adds much to the comfort of all country houses to put in the windows the neat, modern wire-gauze window-guard, which does not obstruct air or sight, and does keep out effectually flies, millers, gnats, beetles, spiders, mosquitoes, bats, cats, and the whole list of nuisances against which we make our rooms close and dismal, and mope in summer evening darkness to avoid. The safety, cleanliness, and comfort of an open country house, night and day, can thus be enjoyed; light, sunshine, and fresh air can be had in abundance, and a feeling of comfort insured which those who have once tried it would never be without.

FIG. 63.—PORTER'S LODGE.

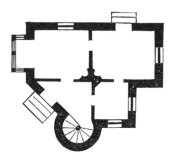

FIG. 64.—GROUND PLAN.

DESIGN No. 21.

PORTER'S LODGE.

BY GEO. E. HARNEY, COLD SPRING, N. Y.

THIS design represents a porter's lodge, built about a year ago by Mr. F. P. James, and situated near the gates at the entrance to his country place in Cold Spring.

It is constructed of rough stone, quarried in the immediate vicinity, laid in its natural bed, and pointed up afterward with light-colored mortar, and—though we object to the use of this light mortar, preferring the softer tint of the dark—the effect of the whole is very good, the bright green foliage of the trees, by which it is nearly hidden, contrasting well with the dark gray tone of the stone.

Its walls are low, and its roof projecting boldly, covered with slates cut in an ornamental pattern. The tower, which is the principal feature of the exterior, rises from the angle of the front nearest the public road, and contains the stairways to the chamber and cellar.

The plan shows four apartments on the principal floor, as follows:

The hall is approached by two or three steps, leading to a wide porch, covered with a broadly projecting hood, supported on heavy brackets. This hood is, in fact, a continuation of the roof of the main house beyond the eaves, as is also the roof of the bay window on the adjoining side.

The staircase in the tower is on the right of the front door, and is separated by an archway from the hall.

The room on the left, containing the bay window, is the living-room, and measures 11 feet 6 inches by 13 feet. It opens into a room 15 feet by 11 feet 6 inches, and is used as a kitchen. The other room is a bedroom, and measures 8 feet by 9 feet. The kitchen has a door communicating with the yard in the rear.

The chimney is in the center of the house, and one stack of three flues answers for all the rooms.

There are ventilators on the roof, and a dormer window to light the attic, which has one room finished off for a sleeping-room. All the principal windows are glazed with diamond-shaped panes of glass.

There is a cellar under the whole house, containing bins for coal, store-closets, etc., etc.

FIG. 65.—WELL-HOUSE.

DESIGN No. 22.

A BARN.

FIG. 66.—A BARN.

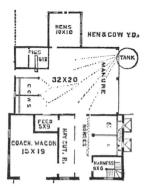

FIG. 67.—GROUND PLAN.

3*

FIG. 68.—A PARSONAGE.

FIG. 69.—CELLAR PLAN.

FIG. 70.—FIRST FLOOR.

FIG. 71.—SECOND FLOOR.

DESIGN No. 23.

A PARSONAGE HOUSE.

THIS design was made for a parsonage house, to be erected in one of the immediate suburbs of New York, and is more commodious than any plan we have thus far shown. The frame to be of the balloon style, sheathed with rough hemlock boards, and covered with narrow siding; roof to be slate, laid in alternate bands of different colors, the lower band to have square ends, the next hexagonal, then square, and so on alternately to the ridge; or shingles may be cut and laid in the same manner. To the top of the first-floor beams the frame should be filled in with brick, to keep out the rats; and if the whole lower floor be grouted between the beams, it would be better and warmer. This is often done to prevent the foul air rising from the cellar through the house. No cellar, however, ought to be foul; ventilate and purify it always; do not have any decaying vegetation in it; grout the floor of the cellar, whitewash the walls and ceiling, and let one open shaft of the chimney start from the cellar. It can be, and should be, at all times sweet and clean. Flooring one inch wide pine; casings, baseboards, etc., to be narrow, neat, and plain; doors 1½ inches in thickness, four paneled; and all interior wood-work to be stained and varnished—not painted. Exterior to be light cream color, with rich, dark-brown trimmings. About New York this house can be erected for $5,000 at present prices of materials and labor.

FIG. 72.

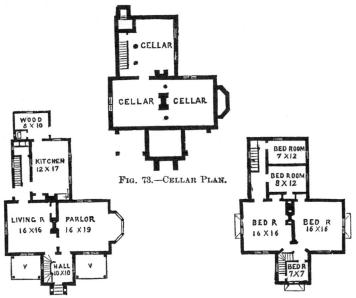

FIG. 73.—CELLAR PLAN.

FIG. 74.—FIRST FLOOR.

FIG. 75.—SECOND FLOOR.

DESIGN No. 24.

THIS design, with a tower, adds a variety to our series, and, in many localities, would be suitable and attractive. The plan shows but moderate accommodation, yet enough to supply the demand called for by the largest number. The roof of the main building can be shingled, but that of the tower would be better of tin. It is shown as a frame house, but would look well constructed of brick; hollow walls, one foot thick; but do not omit furring out. We think there is quite as much need of leaving a vacant space between the plastering and a hollow brick wall as if the wall were solid. The brick which binds a hollow wall will convey dampness, though not as much as solid walls. Our designs are mostly shown as being quite low on the ground. There is nothing arbitrary about this, except that it helps the cottage appearance. In many localities custom or prejudice would raise the foundation wall two or even three feet above the ground. There are some places where it would be healthier and better to do so; but on a dry, gravelly soil, or one thoroughly under-drained, we should not care to show more than a foot of underpinning, unless we contemplated making use of rooms below the first floor.

FIG. 76.

FIG. 77.—CELLAR PLAN.

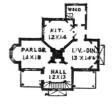

FIG. 78.—FIRST FLOOR.

FIG. 79.—SECOND FLOOR.

DESIGN No. 25.

This design is quite compact, and can be worked out into a very neat and pretty home, and the rooms changed to suit the exposure. Put the hall on the north side, and a south window can be had in three rooms on the first floor and three rooms on the second floor; and if the kitchen wing be extended, and the kitchen removed back, four rooms can, by sliding doors, be thrown together. The ventilation is very perfect, and each room would command good views. For a summer residence, where every breeze is desirable, this would be a good plan; and it is good for many other reasons; it is easily heated, and the housework can be done with few steps.

In the exterior we give, by way of variety, the hipped or truncated gable, a style of finish we do not very much admire, but which will sometimes answer where there is not a disposition to do too much of it. We call to mind a suburban district where one or two leading citizens introduced this notion when it was less common than now, and the fashion thus set has been persistently followed, until it has become quite a disagreeable feature. Make the gables pointed, and this design, both outside and inside, is a good one.

Fig. 80.

Fig. 81.—Cellar Plan.

Fig. 82.—First Floor.

Fig. 83.—Second Floor.

DESIGN No. 26.

CHIMNEYS are an important feature in the exterior design of a dwelling; and we like to see them treated boldly —good solid base, shaft, and projections, and of sufficient height above the roof as to overlook all other obstructions, and thus insure a good draft. The flimsy stove-pipe look of chimney-pots we do not admire, and would prefer not to make use of them. A well-built brick chimney can be put up cheaper, and is much more effective.

In this cottage considerable exterior ornamentation is shown, which may be omitted by those who do not like so much of it. The finials and crest on the roof help the appearance very much, and make a good finish; the drapery on the cornice may be plainer. Hoods over the windows, to some extent, take the place of outside blinds, and relieve, by their shadows, what might otherwise appear to be a very plain exterior.

The rooms, as shown on the plan, would probably be better if increased in size; though, if one undertakes to build low-priced houses, he must adhere firmly to the plan—a little here and a little there will, when all bills are paid, be found to double the cost.

FIG. 84.

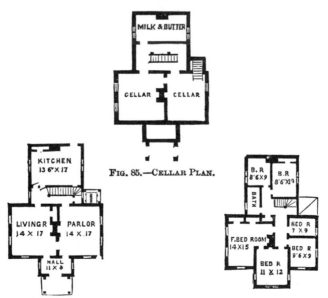

FIG. 85.—CELLAR PLAN.

FIG. 86.—FIRST FLOOR.

FIG. 87.—SECOND FLOOR.

DESIGN No. 27.

WE show here a plain exterior, with a somewhat flatter roof, and full ceilings on the second floor. The bedrooms are all small, and it would probably be better to have a less number, and make them larger, making two rooms out of the four smallest. This roof is what is called one quarter pitch, which is about the flattest that will answer for shingles.

A new roofing material has lately been introduced, called the Mastic Slate, and is highly spoken of by those who have had opportunities to try it. Slate is ground to powder and mixed with gas-works tar, and after being spread with a brush or trowel, becomes in time a sheet of slate. For roofing, it is spread on felting or roofing paper, and the whole expense is very moderate. Our own experience with cheap roofing materials has been quite unsatisfactory, and we have always been glad to exchange them for good tin, shingles, or slate. We would welcome with pleasure the new Mastic Slate, or any other material calculated to reduce the steadily increasing expense of making good, tight, durable roofs. A good material for flat roofs that a farmer can put on himself, is greatly needed.

DESIGNS Nos. 28 and 29.

FIG. 88.—CANOPIED SEAT.

FIG. 89.—A RUSTIC SEAT.

DESIGN No. 30.

MANY persons desire to build to meet present wants, and add at future periods such rooms and accommodations as shall be needed for a growing family or are better adapted to the prosperity to which they look forward. Beginning with very small quarters in this way, one has a home early in life and a savings-bank at the same time, with a double incentive to take care of his surplus earnings. He who begins in this way, and is determined to succeed, will succeed, and gradually become the possessor of a neat and comfortable home, without any greater expenditure than that yearly made by a city tenant for accommodations not any more convenient. It has been well said, "We can not all live out of cities (though it were better for all that many more did so); but even the young merchant, lawyer, doctor, mechanic, or clerk, who feels constrained to live on a paved street, might advantageously own a bit of land, though miles away. Travel is rapid and cheap; a day in the country is health and happiness; and we nearly all hope to live in the country by-and-by. With an acre or more of good land well fenced, the habitual plodder over pavements may plant in youth or early prime the trees that are to solace his old age; may have his plants, shrubs, vines, and fruits growing, though unable as yet to build a house—may have an occasional foretaste of the calm joys of living his own master in his own home. No one can realize all the blessedness which centers in home until he comes to have a spot that is truly his own.

"Thousands live and die tenants and hirelings who might far better employ and house themselves. The city hireling makes more money than his country cousin; but strikes and panics, sickness and frolics, with the necessity of giving half he earns for shelter, generally keep him poor; and an increasing family soon drives him to close calculations and shabby shifts to keep afloat. Happy for him and his, for those he takes with him and those he leaves behind, the day that sees him settled in his own cottage, the owner and occupant of a genuine home!"

FIG. 90.

In fig. 90 we show about the simplest form of a house, containing two rooms, as shown in plans figs. 91, 92.

FIG. 91.—FIRST FLOOR.

FIG. 92.—SECOND FLOOR.

In fig. 93 a simple lean-to addition has been made, and this answers for a kitchen. the plan of which is shown in fig. 94.

FIG. 93.

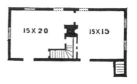

FIG. 94

In·fig. 95 we show the next change, which increases the accommodation and adds to the exterior effect. The plan is shown in fig. 96.

FIG. 95.

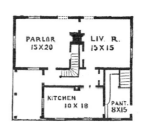

FIG. 96.

FIG. 97.

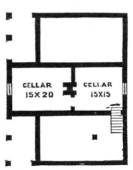

FIG. 98.—CELLAR PLAN.

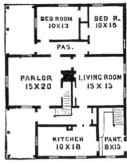

FIG. 99.—FIRST FLOOR.

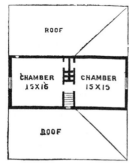

FIG. 100.—SECOND FLOOR.

Fig. 97 shows the final arrangement, with pleasant, well-located, and convenient rooms, and an attractive and pleasing exterior.

Figs. 98, 99, and 100 show the plans as finished — a comfortable home, representing, we will say, what during ten years past might otherwise have gone into a landlord's pocket; and independent of this saving, there has been an annual increase in value, now double the entire expenditure. Time, in its many changes, adds beauty and value to a country home that is taken care of, whose occupants enjoy and are interested in every tree and shrub, and every improvement that is made. Fruits, flowers, and ornamental foliage develop new attractions; and a little done to-day, and a little to-morrow, while being but healthful recreation, amounts to a good deal at the end of a year.

FIG. 101.—DESIGN FOR A FOUNTAIN.

FIG. 102.—SUBURBAN COTTAGE.

FIG. 103.—FIRST FLOOR.

FIG. 104.—SECOND FLOOR.

DESIGN No. 31.

A SUBURBAN COTTAGE.

BY GEO. E. HARNEY, ARCHITECT, COLD SPRING, N. Y.

WE show here a design for a small cottage, such as one might build on a village lot of sixty or a hundred feet in width. It is of frame, filled in with brick—soft brick, laid on edge in mortar—and covered with vertical boarding and battens, or with narrow horizontal siding; the roof covered with shingles cut in patterns; the cellar of rubble-stone; the wall 20 inches thick, laid in mortar.

The frame is of spruce or hemlock (the former is the best, but the latter is the most generally used in this part of the country), and the outside finish of white pine—the details few and simple, but bold and strong—everything meaning something, and telling its own story. The roof is quite steep, and the projection of the eaves broad, to shield the sides, and the windows are all wide and airy.

The accommodation of the house is as follows: A veranda, 6 feet wide, shielding the front entrance. The hall, containing the staircases to the chambers and cellar, and opening into the several rooms on this floor. Parlor, 14 feet by 16, communicating by French casement windows with the veranda on one side, and with an open gallery on the other side, and having, besides, a large hooded mullioned window in the front. This room has, also, what we consider indispensable in a country house, be it large or small—an old fashioned open fire-place, for burning wood on the hearth, if wood can be had, or, if not, coal in the grate, and, besides, for purposes of ventilation. We think, for practical reasons, the old poetic sentiment of the family fireside and the blazing log should not be lost sight of, and there should be at least one room in every house—the room that is the most used by the family as a sitting-room—made attractive and healthy by this means.

The living-room, measuring 13 feet by 15, is provided with two good closets, and opens into a little pantry, which is fitted up with a sink and pump, and other pantry conveniences. This opens out upon a stoop to the yard. There is also on this floor a room 8 feet square, which may be used either as a bed-room or as a store-room; it has no chimney, though if one were added, as easily might be, it could be used as an outer kitchen or scullery.

There is a cellar under the whole house, reached by stairs under the main flight. It is provided with a rain-water cistern, bins for coal, and the other usual cellar conveniences of lock-up—cold cellar, hanging shelves, etc. It has a separate entrance of stone steps from the yard, and is 7 feet high in the clear.

In the second story are chambers corresponding severally with the rooms below, and each supplied with a closet. There is no attic, but an opening in the ceiling of the hall communicates with the vacant space above the rooms, and into it ventilates the house, this space having ventilators under the peaks of the gables.

The front chamber has some importance given to it by the addition of an oriel window, after the fashion of some old English cottages—a feature which adds greatly to the brightness of the room, as well as giving some extra space. It is fitted up with a seat, and has glass windows on its three sides.

The interior of this cottage should be fitted up in simple manner with pine; the closets all supplied with shelves, and hooks, and drawers; and the pantry with sink and other fixtures. The walls may have a hard-finished surface, unless it be contemplated to paper them, in which case a cheaper covering can be used.

The inside wood-work may be stained in two shades with umber and oil; and to add to the effect, the finish for the *best* rooms may be of selected stock, so that the finest and best grained wood may be there used.

The outside should be painted three coats of some neutral colors of oil paint—say light browns, or drabs, or grays. The heights of the stories are 9 feet each. The posts are 14 feet long between sill and plate.

FIG. 105.—HITCHING POST.

DESIGN No. 32.

PLAN FOR LAYING OUT A LOT ONE HUNDRED FEET BY TWO HUNDRED FEET.

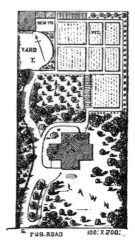

FIG. 106.

A, House.
B, Stable.
T, Turn in Yard.
D, Hot-beds.
H, Grape Arbor.
F, Dwarf and standard fruit-trees.
G, Entrance Gate.
Small fruits in outside border of Vegetable Garden.

DESIGN No. 33.

A TOOL-HOUSE, ETC.

FIG. 107.

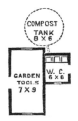

FIG. 108.— PLAN.

DESIGN No. 34.

A PIGGERY.

FIG. 109.

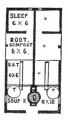

FIG. 110.—PLAN.

This is divided lengthwise through the center, so as to divide different breeds, or young pigs from older ones.

DESIGN No. 35.

SMOKE-HOUSES.

Fig. 111.

Fig. 112.

Fig. 113.—Section.

In fig. 112 the fire is designed to be built in the rear building. The fire is built under a flat stone, to spread the smoke; and the earth on the top of the stone prevents it from radiating heat, as shown in section, fig. 113.

DESIGN No. 36.

PLAN FOR LAYING OUT FIVE ACRES FOR A SUBURBAN VILLA.

BY E. FERRAND, DETROIT. MICH.

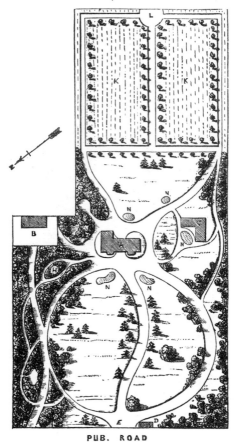

FIG 114.—PLAN.

A, House.	F, Entrance to Barn. [Azaleas.
B, Coach-house, Stable, Yard.	H, Group of Rhododendrons and
C, Greenhouse and Grapery.	K, Kitchen Garden.
D, Gardener's Cottage.	L, Entrance on Street.
E, Principal Entrance.	N, Flower beds.

In this plan, the kitchen garden occupies about 1½ acres.

DESIGN No. 37.

PLAN FOR LAYING OUT AND EMBELLISHING A LOT SEVENTY-
FIVE FEET BY ONE HUNDRED AND FIFTY FEET.

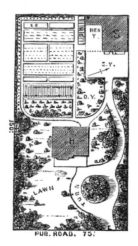

FIG. 115.

H, House.
S, Stable.
A, Fruit-trees on Lawn.
D Y, Drying-yard.
F, Flowers.
S B, Strawberries on the four corners of garden plot.
H B, Hot-beds.

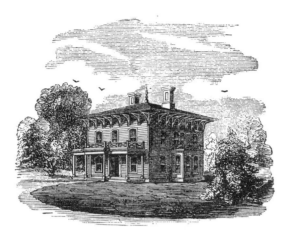

FIG. 116.

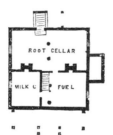

FIG. 117.—CELLAR PLAN.

FIG. 118.—FIRST FLOOR.

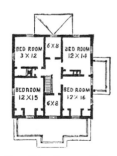

FIG. 119.—SECOND FLOOR.

DESIGN No. 38.

WE show in this design a square house, with the flat or Italian roof, which, for the amount of room obtained, is probably as cheap a style as can be adopted. Projections should all be treated boldly. The location of the house is oftentimes of great importance. It is difficult to persuade those who live in unfrequented districts to place their dwellings back from the road, the passing vehicle or traveler being too acceptable a sight for those who seldom see any one to disturb the loneliness of their situation. In more thickly populated districts this feeling ceases, and a degree of privacy is wished for. As a matter of taste it is better to have a broad and roomy foreground between the house and the street. It gives a finer effect to the house, an opportunity for display in flowers and ornamental trees, greater freedom from noise and dust, and a moderate amount of seclusion.

The great charm of a country home in pleasant weather is its surroundings, and these should always be neatly kept. Roll and cut the lawn regularly; keep the roads and walks in smooth and handsome order; have fine trees, and give them abundant room to grow, and thin out whenever they become crowded. Do not have any more lawn or roadway or walks than can be kept in unexceptionable order. Whatever is done, do well. Better a city lot in fine order than a one-hundred-acre slovenly farm.

Fig. 120.—A Doctor's Residence.

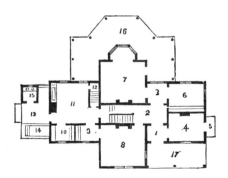

Fig. 121.—Ground Plan.

DESIGN No. 39.

A DOCTOR'S RESIDENCE.

BY G. E. HARNEY, ARCHITECT, COLD SPRING, N. Y.

This design was built about two years ago, by Dr. P. C. Parker, of Cold Spring, and is situated on a fine piece of ground near and overlooking the village, and embracing beyond fine views of the Hudson, West Point, the Newburgh Gap, and the ranges of mountains above and below.

The house stands between the approach road and the river, consequently the entrance porch is on one front— that toward the road—the living apartments and veranda are on the opposite side, fronting the river; by this means greater privacy is given to those portions of the house usually occupied by the family.

The arrangement of the plan is as follows:

The front veranda, No. 17, opens by wide doors into a vestibule, No. 1, 7 feet square; No. 2 is the hall, containing the staircases, and No. 3 is a small room or recess, opening by means of a French window upon the principal veranda, which extends around the river side of the house. The hall and recess are separated from the main hall by Gothic arches with ornamental columns and molded spandrels; No. 4 is the Doctor's business office, which has a separate entrance for persons calling specially on him,

seen at No. 5; No. 6 is a comfortable little library, furnished with book-cases, and having an ornamental chim-
ney-piece ; it has two windows, which give pleasant north
and west views ; No. 7 is a parlor, about 16 feet square,
exclusive of the bay window, which projects from its
western side about 5 feet, and around which the veranda
extends; No. 8 is the dining-room, 15 feet by 16 ; and
No. 9 is a small butler's pantry, fitted up with shelves and
cupboards, and opening into the kitchen, No. 11. The
kitchen is in the southern wing, and is furnished with sink
and other kitchen conveniences; No. 10 is a scullery, fitted
up with cupboards and a sink, and supplied with hot and
cold water; the dishes are washed here, and passed into
the butler's pantry through a small opening left for that
purpose in the wall between them, and on a level with the
wide shelf of the pantry.   A door from the kitchen opens
out upon a private veranda, No. 13, which is entirely shut
in by lattice-work, and this is used in summer as a laundry
or washing-room ; No. 14 is the outside stairway of stone,
leading to the cellar; and No. 15 is a water-closet, made
in a hollow space between two walls, and ventilating
through this space into a flue of the kitchen chimney,
running along by the side of the kitchen flue.   The warmth
of the kitchen flue produces a current of air in the ventilating flue, and by this means the water-closet is fully ventilated, and though quite near the house, is always cleanly
and inoffensive.   Private stairs from the kitchen lead to
the chamber floor and to the cellar.   The cellar has a
laundry under the kitchen, a large store-room under the
butler's pantry, and an open cellar under the rest of the

house, where are the brick cistern, the furnace, coal-bins, wine-closet, and other conveniences usually found in this portion of the house.

In the second story are two square chambers, with full ceilings, over the parlor and dining-room; two rooms for servants, besides a bathing-room over the kitchen; and a stairway to an unfinished attic over the central portion of the house; a chamber over the library, and a large linen room over the office; all these rooms are well lighted and well supplied with closets.

The house is built of wood, filled in with brick, and sided with narrow pine siding; the roofs throughout, including the window hoods, are all covered with slate, put on in alternate bands of green and purple. The interior walls and ceilings are hard-finished, and the interior wood-work is stained and oiled—three different shades being used for the staining — dark umber, light umber, and annatto. The exterior is painted three different shades of oil paint—of browns and grays—and the doors are grained like oak and walnut. The rooms in the principal story are 10 feet high, and those in the chambers are 9 feet high.

Fig. 122.—Design for a Well-House.

DESIGN No. 40.

ICE-HOUSE, COOLING-ROOM, TOOL-HOUSE, AND WORKSHOP
COMBINED.

In this design, the ice is placed in the second story of the main building. The drainage from the ice cools the room below, in which are to be placed meats, fruits, butter, etc. One wing is for a tool-house for farm and garden tools, the other for a workshop. The section is taken lengthwise through the center.

Fig. 123.

Fig. 124.—Plan.

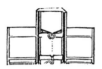

Fig. 125.—Section.

DESIGNS Nos. 41 AND 42.

PLAN FOR LAYING OUT A LOT FIFTY FEET BY ONE HUN-
DRED AND FIFTY FEET.

FIG. 126.

H, House.	D, Dwarf fruit-trees.
E, Entrance.	G, Grape trellis.
O, Hot-beds.	Vegetable Garden in four square plots.

PLAN FOR LAYING OUT AN IRREGULAR PLOT.

FIG. 127.

A, House. S, Stable, etc., at one end of which is Hot-bed. O, Orchard.

FIG. 128.

FIG. 129.—CELLAR PLAN

FIG. 130.—FIRST FLOOR.

FIG. 131.—SECOND FLOOR.

DESIGN No. 43.

A DIFFERENCE of opinion has, and probably always will exist about the materials of which a house should be constructed. We use in this country three leading varieties, wood, brick, and stone, and, to a limited extent, grout and iron. Wood is the cheapest, and if very nice points are considered, is probably the healthiest, certainly the driest. Frame houses have also superior qualities for ventilation, a subject very little understood by those who advocate impenetrable walls and double windows. So little progress has been made in understanding the subject of ventilation, that the commissioners, in advertising for plans for the new Capitol building for the State of New York, mention the necessity of open fire-places for this purpose. Our stone and brick houses, with slate and metal roofs, furnace-heated and air-tight, lack essential qualities for health; while a frame-house, which admits the air more freely, even if it take an extra cord or two of wood, or an extra supply of coal, has a more healthy atmosphere.

Frame houses are good houses, and will outlast the lifetime of the builder; and no matter how strong and substantial a house may be built, it usually passes into strangers' hands at the owner's death.

DESIGN No. 44.

A CHICKEN HOUSE.

FIG. 132.

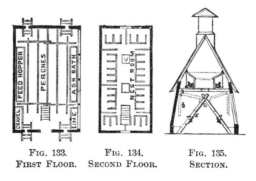

FIG. 133.　　FIG. 134.　　FIG. 135.
FIRST FLOOR.　SECOND FLOOR.　SECTION.

The perches to be laid back against the walls when cleaning out.

DESIGN No. 45.

PLAN FOR LAYING OUT A LOT ONE HUNDRED AND FIFTY
FEET BY TWO HUNDRED FEET.

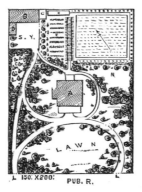

Fig. 130.

A, House.
B, Stable.
D, Henery.
C, Manure Pit.
S Y, Stable Yard.
H, Hot-beds.
G, Dwarf fruit.
N, Drying-yard.
F, Raspberries, along one side of which is a grape arbor covering
    the walk.
LL, Entrances.
    Currant and other small fruits around outside border.

DESIGN No. 46.

A BARN.

Fig. 137.

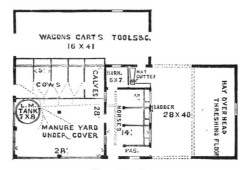

Fig. 138.—Plan.

DESIGN No. 47.

PLAN FOR LAYING OUT A PLOT OF ABOUT TWO ACRES.

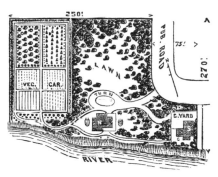

Fig. 139.

H, House.
S, Stable, etc.
C, Hen Yard.
O, Standard Fruits.
D, Dwarf Fruits.
Blackberries all around the garden.
Currants, etc., around fruit plots.

DESIGN No. 48.

HOW TO REMODEL AN OLD HOUSE.

FIG. 140.—THE OLD HOUSE.

FIG. 141.—CELLAR PLAN.

FIG. 142.—FIRST FLOOR.

Fig. 143.—Second Floor.   Fig. 144.—Garret.

WE show here what can be done with an old house—one built by a retiring citizen, and modeled after his city residence, under the impression, perhaps, it was equally well adapted for the broad open country. We know of many a one who has saved in this manner architect's fees; but such houses sooner or later become subjects for the architect's skill, and not unfrequently a good thing can be made out of them.

Fig. 140 shows the appearance of the old house and the four plans of basement, first floor, second floor, and garret, as they were originally laid out. It is the same thing a thousand times repeated, in almost every densely populated street; every discomfort of a city house, with the interminable stairways, has been transported to the country.

In fig. 145 we show the new design for modernizing, in a tasteful manner, this clumsy exterior. By an addition we give more room upon the two principal floors, so that even a moderate-sized family may abandon, for their own

FIG. 145.—THE OLD HOUSE REMODELED.

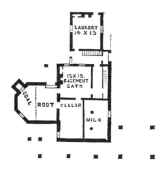

FIG. 146.—CELLAR PLAN.

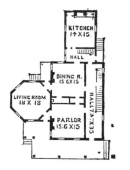

FIG. 147.—FIRST FLOOR.

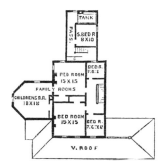

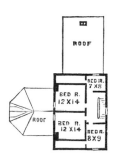

FIG. 148.—SECOND FLOOR.   FIG. 149.—GARRET.

use, both basement and garret. A broad and spacious veranda, with *porte cochere* at one end, adds greatly to the outside enjoyment and appearance, and the exterior outline and shadow so managed as to make a pleasing impression. The grounds and other surroundings have also been differently planned; a handsomely curved line of roadway takes the place of the straight-line communication with the highway. The orchard of apple-trees which surrounds the house will be thinned out and planted up with ornamental trees, thus breaking up the parallel lines. The lawn in front is to be kept smooth, clean, and handsome, and all the awkward stiffness of house, grounds, and shrubbery changed to the graceful ease of an inviting country house with a neat and spacious foreground. All this is accomplished with a small expenditure of money, which, however, might have been saved on the start by one wise enough to employ the proper talent to aid him in the design.

DESIGN No. 49.

PLAN FOR LAYING OUT A LOT OF ONE ACRE.

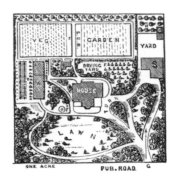

FIG. 150.

S, Stable and Barn.

A, Greenhouse and Grapery.

O, Double Henery.

H, Hen Yard, set with fruit-trees.

D, Grape Arbor, between which and Greenhouse is a row of dwarf
fruit-trees.

I, Dwarf and Standard fruit-trees and currants.

F, Fountain.

J, Flowers

O, Water-closet and Garden Tool-house in rear.

E, Dwarf fruit-trees.

DESIGN No. 50.

PLAN FOR LAYING OUT A LOT OF TWO ACRES.

FIG. 151.

A, House.

E, Entrance.

B, Stables and Carriage-house.

D, Greenhouse and Grapery.

I, Henery, with double yard, C C, containing a few fruit-trees.

S B, Strawberries.

R B, Raspberries.

V, Dwarf Orchard.

O, Standard Orchard.

Grapes between Greenhouse and Stables.

Surrounding border of Garden set with blackberries.

COMPUTING COST.

A SIMPLE and rapid plan for estimating the cost of any building is by comparison. If carefully done, it will give figures that may be relied on. We have said before that it would be productive of much mischief to name prices in a book like this. The only prices we could give would be local ones, and these are changing here every day. We were of this opinion when we prepared " Woodward's Country Homes," a book that has met with extraordinary success, and has been ordered from every quarter of the globe; and experience thus far confirms us in the belief that the opinion then formed was correct.

The best substitute for prices, on which confidence may be placed, is the following, a plan much used by builders to test the accuracy of their detail estimates :

We will suppose that a party desires to erect a building in the vicinity of Madison, Wis., where prices of materials and labor differ largely from New York prices. Let him select such a house already built in that vicinity as shall represent, in style of architecture and character of finish, about what he desires to construct, and of which the cost of building is known; then compute the area or number of square feet covered by the building; divide the number of dollars of cost by the number of square feet thus found, and the price per square foot is ascertained.

Thus a house 40 feet by 40 feet covers an area of 1,600 square feet; it costs $8,000; and dividing $8,000 by 1,600, shows $5 per square foot. Now what will be the cost of a similar house covering 1,400 square feet?

$$1,400 \times \$5 = \$7,000.$$

This plan will do very well to approximate roughly to cost. A better and closer one is to ascertain the cost per cubic foot. Thus, a house 40 feet by 40 feet, and an average height of 30 feet. $40 \times 40 \times 30 = 48,000$ cubic feet, cost $7,200, or fifteen cents per cubic feet. Then a house containing 57,000 cubic feet, at fifteen cents, would cost $8,550. Where all conditions of comparison are equal, such as equal facilities for buying, equal advantages in capital, credit, good management, etc., one can very closely by, this last method, ascertain about the cost of such a building as he proposes to erect.

FIG. 152.—DESIGN FOR GATEWAY.

FIG. 153.

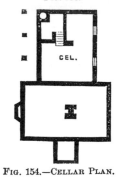

FIG. 154.—CELLAR PLAN.

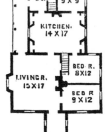

FIG. 155.—FIRST FLOOR.

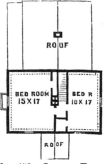

FIG. 156.—SECOND FLOOR.

DESIGN No. 51.

THIS cottage shows a somewhat different construction outside from those already given, and although it adds somewhat to the expense, gives more variety.

Such a plan as this can be added to advantageously whenever desirable to do so. Indeed, most of the plans given admit of additions; and one advantage of the Rural Gothic style is, that every wing put on increases the exterior effect. Add almost anything in keeping with the original structure, let the roofs be on different levels, and the building will assume the appearance of a pile of buildings, irregular in outline and prolific in beauties of light and shadow.

Finish the walls with two coats of mortar and one coat of hard finish; on the lower floor put in a simple cornice, and omit all plaster ornaments. Stain and oil or varnish all interior wood-work; do not paint any room but the kitchen. In this manner you can get a warm and pleasing effect, and have the wood-work always free from dirt. Good effects can be produced by staining moldings and panels to resemble different varieties of wood; or our native hard woods can be used with fine effect, if expense is not considered. It may not generally be known that all mahogany and rosewood furniture is stained, the natural wood being very much lighter in color.

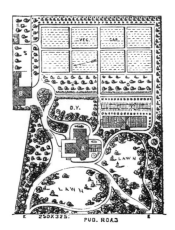

FIG. 157.

A, House.
C, Conservatory, side of house.
B, Stable, Carriage-house, etc.
D, Henery, with double yard, S S, set in plants.
D Y, Drying-yard.
G, Grapery and Greenhouse.
F, Fountain.
E E, Entrance Gates.
T, Grape Trellis.
O O, Orchard.
    Fruit around garden.

DESIGN No. 52.

PLAN FOR LAYING OUT A LOT TWO HUNDRED AND FIFTY FEET BY THREE HUNDRED AND TWENTY-FIVE FEET.

THE lot for which this design was made had one side irregular, as shown, but the planting has been so managed that no one would suspect that such an abruptness existed. Two separate lawns are shown, divided by the carriage drive. The lawns are planted on their outer edges, but are better open and clear from all shrubbery in the interior. They should, throughout the growing season, be closely mown at least every two weeks. The drive from street to house should be 10 feet wide, and finished with a hard, smooth, and evenly graded surface, and kept free from weeds; edges of lawn to be trimmed neatly as often as required. Whatever is done in the way of ornamental grounds should be well done. Nothing looks so shabby as neglected walks and overgrown lawns; better not make any attempt to lay out the grounds tastefully, unless there is a disposition to keep them neat and well ordered. The stable is planted out in such a manner as not to be seen from the house, and the general arrangement of the grounds is such as will make them attractive and convenient. The lot contains about two acres, abundantly large for one whose business is elsewhere. No one need ever be in want of occupation for his leisure hours when he has two acres to embellish and see to its neat keeping.

DESIGN No. 53.

A BARN.

FIG. 158.

FIG. 159.—FIRST FLOOR.

FIG. 160.—SECOND FLOOR.

DESIGN No. 54.

A FARM COTTAGE.

Fig. 161.

Fig. 162.
CELLAR PLAN.

Fig. 163.
FIRST FLOOR.

Fig. 164.
SECOND FLOOR.

FIG. 165.—A FARM-HOUSE.

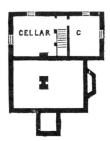

FIG. 166,—CELLAR PLAN.

FIG. 167.—FIRST FLOOR.

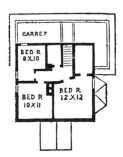

FIG. 168.—SECOND FLOOR.

DESIGN No. 55.

A FARM-HOUSE.

THIS design shows a neat and compact farm-house, covered by a plain roof, without hips or valleys, with a number of conveniently arranged, but not very large, bed-rooms. It must be understood that these designs, in all cases, admit of many changes; that is, rooms may be made larger or smaller, and increased or decreased in number; the exterior in one design may be used for the ground-plan of another, or the good points of several plans may be collected and an entirely new plan re-arranged from them, and an exterior adapted to it. In all designs shown, the perspective view is adapted to the plans connected with it; and in making changes there are many points to be thoroughly considered. In some instances it would be necessary to reverse the plan; that is, change the location of rooms from one side to the other, in order to take advantage of the exposure.

That we should succeed in meeting in all respects the wishes of any one person, we do not expect; yet repeated instances have come to our knowledge of buildings having been put up in exact accordance with our published plans. We believe, however, that we do give every one who contemplates building, suggestions and plans of great value, and one can, with a little ingenuity, adapt the hints to suit his own peculiarities.

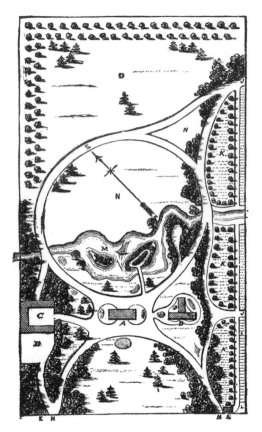

FIG. 169.—PLAN.

A, Dwellin
B, Greenhouses and Graperies.
C, Stable, Barn, and Interior Yard.
D, Yard.
E, F, Gardeners' Houses.
H, Principal Entrances.

J, Entrances.
K, Vegetable Garden.
L, Hot-beds.
M, River, Lake, and Islands.
N, Meadow.
O, Fields, with two rows of
apple-trees.

DESIGN No. 56.

PLAN FOR LAYING OUT A TEN-ACRE LOT FOR SUBURBAN OCCUPATION.

BY E. FERRAND, DETROIT, MICH.

THIS place has two main entrances, with well-shaded drives. The lodges for the gardeners command the gates. There is an immediate access from one of these cottages to the hot-beds and garden, which are exposed to the full sun. The sight of the vegetable garden is entirely hidden by a belt of ornamental planting. Around the green-house and graperies are flower-beds and rustic seats, with a nice walk around. Rhododendrons and kalmias can be planted on the northern and other shaded sides of the dwelling. The access is very easy to the stables and other out-buildings, with two yards and a direct access to the street. The river and lake occupy about half an acre. There are two islands, one of which is connected with the garden by a small bridge. The space O can be cultivated with fruits of any kind, or put in grass.

It has been my aim to make this a handsome place, with but few roads. In fact, a simple glance at the drawing will tell more about the disposition of this place than any explanation.

Fig. 170.—A School-House.

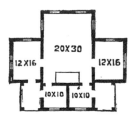

Fig. 171.—Ground Plan.

DESIGN No. 57.

A COUNTRY SCHOOL-HOUSE.

BY GEO. E. HARNEY, ARCHITECT, COLD SPRING, N. Y.

WE present at this time a sketch of a country school-house, of suitable size and accommodation for about fifty pupils, of both sexes.

It is a plain building of wood, comprising a central portion and two wings, one on each side. The main building measures 21 feet by 42, and the wings 12 by 17 each. The principal school-room measures 20 feet by 30, and is 12 feet high to the spring of the ceiling, and 17 feet high in the center of the room, the ceiling for a portion of the way following the slant of the rafters, and the principal rafters and braces projecting out so as to show from below. The walls of this room are wainscoted up to the level of the window-sills—4 feet from the floor — with narrow ceiling boards, and above that, together with the ceiling, are finished off with a rough and stucco finish.

The wood-work should all be stained, and the walls tinted some soft neutral tint — gray, or cream, or pearl color.

The windows are all sash windows, double-hung for purposes of ventilation; and, in addition, there are two ventilating shafts rising from the floor through the attic, and terminating in the ventilator on the ridge of the main roof. These shafts have openings near the floor and ceiling, with arrangements for opening and shutting at will. They are made of smoothly-planed, well-jointed pine boards, and measure each 16 inches square inside.

In order to keep up the circulation, and to supply cool air from outside, a shaft is introduced running along under the floor, and terminating at the platform on which, in winter, the stove, or heating-apparatus, will stand, and from this distributed into the room by numerous small holes in the riser of the platform.

We consider the simplest methods of ventilation the best, and the above will be found both simple and effective. The great desideratum is to provide means for the discharge of a certain quantity of vitiated air, and to supply its place by the same quantity of pure air, properly warmed in winter. To make the discharge more effective, the stove-pipe may be carried up in connection with one of the shafts, rarefying the air, and making the upward current stronger; but in ordinary cases this will be hardly necessary.

There are two entrances to this house, one for boys and one for girls. Both entries are 10 feet square, and are in the main building, opening directly into the school-room.

The wing on the right is a class-room, and that on the left is designed for wood and coal, and for a wash-room, if such be considered desirable.

The entries, instead of having hooks for clothing, have each a sufficient number of boxes or shelves divided up into compartments of about two cubic feet each, ranged along the sides, and carried up in three or four tiers. These boxes are all numbered, and each scholar has one for his own exclusive use; being provided with a duplicate number as a voucher, there is no opportunity for contention as to ownership, no losing or abusing of hats and shawls, and dinner-pail. The method has been tried, and found much preferable to the old arrangements of hooks, particularly for the smaller scholars, and those coming from a distance who bring their dinners.

The two porticoes measure 8 feet by 10; the windows have all broad hoods and brackets; the gables have heavy finials, and the ridge is surmounted by a large ventilator. The roofs are covered with slates, and the walls are painted two or three coats of oil paint.

Fig. 172.- Design for Entrance Gate.

DESIGN No. 58.—A GRAPE ARBOR.

BY E. A. BAUMANN.

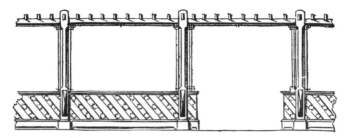

FIG. 173.—SIDE VIEW OF ARBOR.

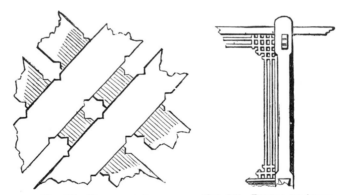

FIG. 174.—DETAIL OF ARBOR.   FIG. 175.—DETAIL OF ARBOR.

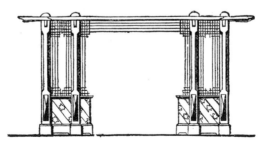

FIG 176.—CROSS SECTION.

DESIGN FOR A GRAPE ARBOR.

THE accompanying design for a grape arbor, in the style of an Italian pergola, has been introduced in several places with success.

This arbor is more an ornament to a place than arbors generally, which are intended more to hide nuisances, but which show them in the best way to everybody that comes near a house.

By the design, it will be seen that the arbor is open on the front side, with a balustrade or panel work of 3½ or 4 feet high from the ground.

The rear is covered with laths, 12 to 15 inches apart, for the purpose of training grapevines intended to run on the top, along the cross-pieces.

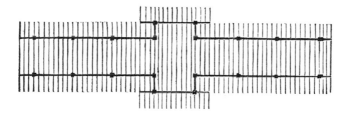

FIG. 177.—TOP OF ARBOR.

This arbor could be built of almost any kind of timber, and painted any shade; but a wood color, imitating oak or chestnut, would be the most suitable.

The upright lattice-work, running along the posts, is intended to give the posts a heavier appearance, and to tie up flowering climbers that will have to be trained lengthwise along the upper piece of timber.

The horizontal pieces run across the posts, tying them together and supporting the laths, 2½ by 3½ inches, which are lying crosswise over them, and project some 15 to 18 inches out.

Vines dropping from the top will soon make the whole more heavy.

When first employed or introduced, this style of arbor was either to shut out some objects outside the place, on parts of a small lot, where a group or a belt of shrubbery would not have found room enough, or to establish an ornamental terminus in the pleasure ground, and a separation between this and the vegetable garden.

With a well-selected collection of climbers, this arbor would soon be a very handsome feature in a place. Tall-growing varieties of climbers, like wistarias, clematis, running roses, etc., may be trained on the posts; and dwarfer sorts, like honeysuckles, akebia, bignonias, jasminums, the annual varieties of ipomæas, tropæolums, etc., may be employed along the base.

In case this arbor should be placed on the boundary line of a place, the rear on the north side would not answer well for grapevines; but in that case, I should suggest to cover the rear entirely with the Virginia creeper, aristolochia sipho, or some other fast-growing climber succeeding well in the shade.

WITHIN DOORS.

[THE following hints were originally published in the HORTICULTURIST. They were written by Dr. D. D. Slade, of Boston, Mass., and we commend them for their sound teachings.]

It is not alone to the outward embellishment of the country home that art and taste should be directed. The influence of these should be shown as well in its internal arrangement and adornment, and that, too, in a way to conduce to the welfare and happiness of the family, and indirectly to promote that genial, unrestrained sociability which should ever characterize country life. To the full accomplishment of this, our rural communities, possessed as they are of ample means, need only to have their good sense and judgment properly directed. Toward this end but little has as yet been said or done, while, on the contrary, much thought has been given to rural embellishment in the usual acceptation of the term.

How can we hope to effect that which is so much to be desired? How can we best make known the necessary suggestions to those who might profit by them? We can have no better means than those which the pages of the HORTICULTURIST present.

There are certain little foibles, of which our country neighbors, particularly in New England, are guilty, which we heartily wish were abolished. For example, we would that the spirit, not always to be attributed to meanness, were done away with, which shuts up every portion of the dwelling, even against its own inmates, excepting perhaps a single apartment. In that delightful book, " My Farm at Edgewood," the author gives us a faithful picture of this failing too commonly met with; and the death of poor Dorothy, and the opening of the darkened parlors, is a true sketch of what takes place every day in almost every country village.

We would gladly see the money now expended in the trashy, half-made articles of furniture, merely because the uncomfortable shapes of some of them are said to be of the latest style, laid out for those which are truly strong and serviceable, and, for this reason, elegant.

We grieve to know that there are families who would willingly dispose of ancestral relics—choice heirlooms that they are, in the shape of solid mahogany chairs, lofty chests of drawers with curiously-wrought brass handles, elaborately carved bureaus, claw-footed tables, etc., all in perfect preservation, and all of which would long outlive their present owners, as they have their preceding ones—to supply their places with modern articles, with chairs and sofas upon which no mortal man could ever sit or recline with the least degree of comfort, and with beds and bureaus which soon melt away before the blasts of our modern stoves and furnaces.

We would wish that less dependence were placed in these very stoves and furnaces, and that an open fire-place existed in every room, thus securing ample ventilation and cheerfulness, and thereby contributing to good health and happiness. That at the proper seasons every blind and curtain in the country home should be thrown open to ad-

mit the genial sunlight. That the light from the blazing
wood-fire, as it dances on the walls and ceiling, should
show to the belated traveler as he passes, the forms of a
happy group gathered about the ample chimney place.

These are but a tithe of the changes which would exert
ourselves to bring about among the intelligent of our rural
population. As regards the arrangement and adornment
of the interior of the country dwelling, we shall speak
more especially of the dining-room.

There is nothing more essential to the comfort, and consequently to the happiness, of the family, than that the
dining-room should be, of all the apartments of the house,
the most pleasant and the most attractive. And to this
end, the first requisite is, that it should be properly
placed. In building, or in the occupation of the residence
already constructed, let that room be selected for the purpose into which the morning sun at least shall throw its
cheerful rays. In our cold climate, at no time is its
presence more welcome than at the breakfast-table. If
practicable, let both the morning and evening sunlight
illuminate the room. These points can be attained by the
choice of the southeastern exposure. It is not uncommon-
ly the case, that the most dreary, forbidding room in the
house has been chosen for the daily repasts—a room into
which no sunshine ever pours, and whose whole aspect
partakes of that gloomy spirit which too often broods over
the tables of our people. We are great advocates for the
admission of the sun, especially into those rooms which
are occupied throughout the day, and in the construction of a country dwelling, where choice of position is

almost invariably to be had, this important point is to be kept most distinctly in view. Where his beams penetrate, household neglect on the part of mistress or dependents is not so apt to be tolerated.

And who can estimate the moral influence which a cheerful, sunlighted, tastefully-arranged room exerts over the members of a household, especially over the younger portion? An influence which shall go with them through life, and which shall build up happy associations, to which their minds shall ever joyfully revert, wherever in the broad world may be their habitation.

In the picture which we should form of what a dining-room ought to be, certainly so far as regards the essential points of which we have spoken, we can not do better than to present a description of our own, for to us at least it embodies all that is requisite for the growth and encouragement of that home-feeling which we would ever see manifested in our children.

We have a decided penchant for all that smacks of antiquity. We like old houses and old furniture, particularly if comely and serviceable. We delight in painting to ourselves the scenes through which they must have passed; we believe, too, that they exert a much greater influence in producing a love for home than those constructed at a more recent period. Having premised thus much, we will say that our house is old, with a gambrel roof; that its location is a delightful one; that we have refined and agreeable neighbors, and those not too near. The dining-room has a bay-window to the southeast, and two windows with a southerly aspect. The morning and evening sun throughout the year gladdens it with its presence. The apartment is of fair dimensions, the ceiling low—so low, that in the moments of play and during temporary forgetfulness we have brought the heads of our children into very dangerous proximity.

The principal feature of the room, and the one in which we take the most delight, is the big open fire-place, which will admit as large a log as one can conveniently bring in. The back and jambs are of brick, well blackened with the soot of many a generous fire. The tiled hearth is broad and long; well-polished brass andirons and fenders, with the accompanying shovel, tongs, and bellows, all necessary appendages to the fire on the hearth, are each in their appropriate places.

And what would induce us to part with the cheery and happy spirit which this old fire-place continually infuses into our little family—whether at the morning hour, when we first assemble around the table, or at the " children's hour," between daylight and dark, when we gather around its hearth to listen to some oft-read story or to recite some well-known adventure! A Turkey carpet of pleasing colors and of thick texture, an article which, in our minds, is always associated with substantial old-fashioned families, contributes greatly to our comfort. An antique sideboard, convenient both in its external and internal arrangements, with a half dozen high-backed mahogany chairs, telling of Dutchland, not to forget a more luxurious armchair, constitute the movable furniture. Simple, unostentatious woolen curtains hang at the bay and other windows, supported upon black walnut fixtures. These may be easily dropped at night, shutting off, if necessary, the recess of the bay-window, and thereby adding amazingly to the cosy, secure feeling in which we love to indulge in the long winter evenings of the country. Numerous engravings adorn the wall, not in gilded frames, but in those made of hard wood, merely polished and not varnished, and simple in design. Beside the ancient clock and bronze candlesticks, numerous little objects, tokens of kind remembrance, adorn the broad and ample mantle-shelf. Plants, whose flowers have delighted us through the dreary season of winter, find a congenial atmosphere and plenty of sunlight in the bay-window. It is hardly necessary to state that a convenient pantry and a good closet, adjuncts which can not be dispensed with in the well-ordered household, are contiguous.

Such are the principal features of our dining-room. While we have seen many that are more spacious and elegant, we have rarely seen any that contained within it more that was essential to comfort or that was more calculated to make a stranger feel at home.

We have been thus particular in our description, for the reason that we would dilate more fully upon certain points.

Of course, we could not hope to govern all tastes, but in such a matter as the selection of a carpet for a country dining-room, we should advocate the choice of one modest, not only in color, but in design. So also with the coloring of the walls, whether by paint or paper, we should be governed by similar rules of fitness—giving our preference to some warm neutral tint, and most decidedly eschewing white, as a color totally unfitted for either adornment of exterior or interior.

Drapery curtains, however simple in their fabric or construction, contribute greatly to the appearance of a room, doing away with that bareness which is never agreeable, at least during the cold season. For their accompanying fixtures, the various species of hard wood simply polished are far preferable to the gilded, which are less suitable in the country, being more tawdry and more easily destroyed. The same remarks apply also to the frames of engravings, and in many cases even those of oil paintings. These may seem to be matters of trifling importance, but they all go to show the presence of good sense and a refined taste ruling over a household.

Plants, whether upon a stand or hanging in appropriate pots at the window, add amazingly to the cheerfulness of any room, contributing to the pleasure of those who care and tend for them. They serve also as useful barometers, telling us, by their condition, of the atmospherical state of our apartments, their delicate organization being unable to stand against the injurious emanation from overheated furnaces. Mr. Rand, in his pleasant book upon flowers, says, " A plant or a stand of flowers is a constant source of pleasure in a room ; it is a spring of sunshine, and its silent influence makes all the household more cheerful and better."

Finally, a certain degree of harmony should be preserved in all that concerns the internal embellishment of the country home, a point which is very apt to be overlooked by those otherwise correct in their tastes.

TRACING CURVED LINES FOR ROADS,
WALKS, Etc.

a, *b*, *c*, being a tangent or straight line, from the point *b* we proceed to lay out a curved line; 5 feet from *b*, at *d*, lay off the distance 6 inches, and set the stake at 1, 5 feet from *b*, and 6 inches from *d*. Then from *b*, through 1, produce the straight line to *e*; 5 feet from station 1 lay off the deflection distance, 12 inches, and set the stake 2 5 feet from 1, and 12 inches from *e*. Then repeat the same operation, setting stakes 3 and 4, all of which will be found to be in the arc of a circle. If the wish is to pass into a tangent or straight line, the next distance will be but 6 inches, or the first and last distances in running from and on to a tangent are always half the others, and are usually called tangential distances. To sharpen the curve, lay off in the same direction from the tangent already found on the first curve, any tangential distance greater than 6 inches, which in this case we make 9 inches, and set stake No. 5. Then produce the straight line from stake 4 through stake 5 to *f*, and lay off the deflection distance 18 inches to stake 6. Set stake 7 in the same manner; then run on to a tangent by setting off ½ the deflection distance at station 8, and producing a straight line from stake No. 7. At station 7 we reverse the curve. From the tangent of the curve just run, lay off, on the opposite side, the tangential distance 6 inches, and set station 8; then produce the line from 7 through 8 to *g*, and lay off the deflection distance 12 inches from *g*, and set station 9; then produce the line from 8 through 9 to *h*, and lay off 12 inches to

station 10 ; then produce the line from 9 through 10 to *i*,
and lay off the tangential distance 6 inches, and set stake
11. The line from 10 through 11, and continued, is the
tangent from which, at any point on either side, curves can
be laid out. All the stations are equidistant. Each curve

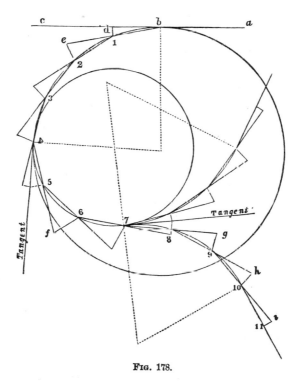

Fig. 178.

begins and ends on a tangent. Where a curve compounds
or reverses, the tangent is common to both. A tangent or
straight line may be introduced between curves running
in an opposite or similar direction, but curves running one
way should join each other. It is bad taste to put a tan-

gent between them, if there is any way to avoid it. A tangent between reverse curves improves their appearance.

This principle of tracing curves is very simple and rapid, and requires no revision to ascertain if they flow gracefully and correctly. There is no necessity for clearing the ground, removing fences or other obstructions, as the line can be continued whenever two stakes can be seen. Mathematically speaking, there is a very slight difference to be detected in demonstrating this problem. In practice, however, this trivial difference can hardly be said to cause any departure from absolute accuracy. We merely mention this lest some hypercritical theorist might think he had discovered something.

An expert, familiar with this process, has a wonderful facility in executing work, while those who work by the eye only will remain in the background. He does at once what they spend hours or days to attain, as the same harmony and grace of line is the object of both.

A measuring tape and rule and a plumb-line, or a couple of light thin rods, are all the instruments necessary to do the work. It requires considerable practice to select the proper curve at first, but one or two trials will give the right deflection distances. Trial lines of this kind, we find, enable us to ascertain in the easiest and quickest manner the proper radius of a curve, without the necessity of making an instrumental survey. As a matter of economy and beauty, this system recommends itself strongly; and in a very extensive professional practice we have found its merits above all others.

DESIGN No. 59.

It frequently happens that a plan is called for which will admit of future additions, as family and fortune increase. Many are deterred from building in consequence of the expense of building on a larger scale than their necessities require, and are hardly willing to put up a structure to be torn down a ew years after. But if a house adapted to present wants can be had, and hereafter become a useful and harmonious portion of a more commodious dwelling, the objection named is obviated. In the city, one's social position is regulated as much by the house he lives in as by the company he keeps or the clothes he wears. In the country, let one live in ever so humble a cottage and his position is not altered by it. If furnished and embellished in good taste, it rather advances the position than otherwise. Real, substantial comfort in country life will always take precedence of any attempt at show.

The accompanying design shows a cottage of moderate pretensions, and which can be erected at the present time (April, 1868,) in the suburbs of New York for $1,500 to $1,800. The kitchen is designed to be in the basement, with cellar, and a small laundry adjoining. The amount of room on first and second floors is shown on the plans. The frame is to be built in the Balloon style, which is the strongest and cheapest, and may be filled in

FIG. 179.—COTTAGE.

with soft brick on edge, or double boarded and interlaid with roofing felt. The main roof to be of slate, and if of small sizes and cut to hexagon pattern, would have a pretty effect. Our taste would be to use one color only, the dark blue. Slate roofs cost but a trifle more than shingles, and the rain water is so clear and beautiful as to render well or spring water unnecessary. Piazza and bay window roofs to be tinned, and gutters and leaders from all roofs to a cistern. Exterior finish to be plain, good and substantial, and to be painted a light cream or warm gray tint, with rich brown trimmings. The walls throughout to be hard finished white, and after a year or two to be papered.

The first plans of the house are shown by the dark lines; the addition to be put up at some future day is indicated by the light lines. When this is done, it is intended to remove the stairs shown, make the necessary alterations in partitions, etc, and use the entire present hall and dining-room for an enlarged platform stairway, vestibule, hat-closet, etc., with an arched lobby communicating from vestibule to future parlor. The present parlor will become the future dining-room, communicating directly with kitchen through waiter's pantry " D." The present front-door opening will be enlarged to correspond with the double window and folding doors substituted. The closet in the rear will become a lobby, communicating with future kitchen, and through new lobby " E " with future library " F."

The index letters on the plan of the addition indicate future rooms, etc., respectively, as follows:

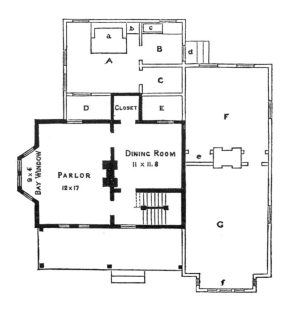

FIG. 180.—PLAN FIRST FLOOR.

FIRST STORY.

A, Kitchen............size, 12 x 12 feet.   *a*, Kitchen Range,
B, Wash-room......... "   7 x 7   "   *b*, Boiler.
C, Kitchen Pantry..... "   7 x 4½ "   *c*, Sink.
D, Waiter's   "   ..... "   7 x 4   "   *d*, Outside Steps.
E, Lobby, 4 feet wide.   *e*, Book Closet.
F, Library............. "   14 x 14   "
G, Parlor............. "   14 x 18   "
    With Bay Window.. "   9 x 2½   "

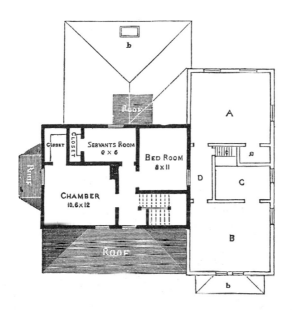

FIG. 181.—PLAN SECOND FLOOR.

SECOND STORY.

A, Chamber .... size, 14 x 12 feet. a, Closet.
B,   "   .... "   14 x 12   "   b b, Roofs.
C, Dressing-Room...... "   6 x 9½   "   c, Attic Stairs.
D, Lobby, 4 feet wide.

Fig. 182.—French Roof Cottage.

DESIGN No. 60.

THE French roof is very popular in almost all sections, gives more available space than the gothic, and when well managed is effective in appearance. The design shown contemplates a moderate expenditure; and in this,

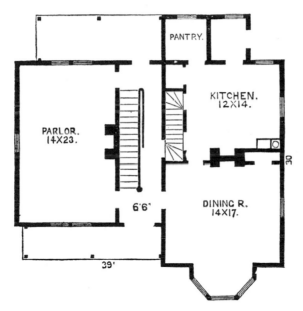

FIG. 183.—PLAN FIRST FLOOR.

as in the previous design, part of the work is to be left for future completion. By omitting the finish of the attic and constructing the building in a good but plain manner the cost should not exceed $3,800. This price would provide but one mantel for the parlor, and does

not contemplate either heating or plumbing. The cellar
ceiling to be 7 feet; first floor ceiling, 10 feet; second,
9 feet; and attic, 9 feet; the deck-roof to be tin and the
lower roof to be of slate. The attic plan is given to
show the arrangement, and can be finished at any future
time. This plan would answer well for a suburban
lot 50 feet front, and will be found to meet most of the

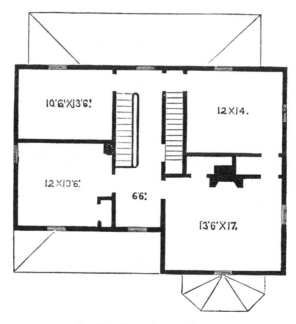

FIG. 184.—PLAN SECOND FLOOR.

requirements of a country house. The hall, through the
centre, gives independent access to all rooms, and affords
thorough ventilation in warm weather. The parlor is
amply large for all purposes, and the general situation of
the rooms is such that they can be economically heated.

In the preparation of house plans, nothing pays so well as careful study. Ten per cent., and sometimes as much as twenty per cent. of the cost of the house can be saved by skillful treatment in construction and arrangement. Cheap plans are the most expensive portions of house-building, and generally more profitable to make

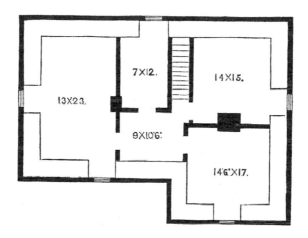

FIG. 185.—PLAN ATTIC FLOOR.

than those on which the most thorough care and study have been expended, and for which the customary price for good work has been paid. Better bestow more thought and more money on the plan, and get the best house possible for the price contemplated.

DESIGN No. 61.

THE design for this house was prepared to answer a popular demand, that shall embrace, at a low price, the long-prized excellencies of the old-fashioned country

FIG. 186.—GOTHIC COTTAGE.

house, with hall through the centre and doors at both ends to give ample ventilation in warm weather. With all the progress that has been made in architectural con-

venience and embellishments, we doubt if the central
hall and independent communication with all rooms have
been much improved on.   The finest country houses with
which our associations are connected, and which are
remembered for their comfort and elegance, had the
spacious hall running through the centre.

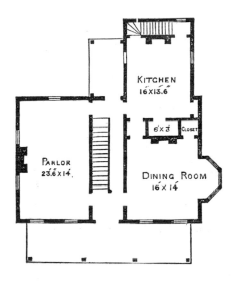

FIG. 187.—PLAN FIRST FLOOR.

It will be observed in this design, that as far as possible all angles have been avoided, and the construction
planned for straight-forward square work.   The roof of
the addition is nearly flat and tinned, and the ridge
finished below the plate of main roof.   The principal
roof is covered with slate, cut to hexagonal pattern, has
a square pitch, and except the connection with central

gablet, is without vallies; the rooms are pleasantly located, easily reached, and for economy are as compact as
any plan that may be devised of similar area. The
exterior is plain, but, at the same time, it looks well, and
will wear well, and while without the irregularities that
afford variety of light and shade, it is also without the
expense connected with them. By omitting the bay win-

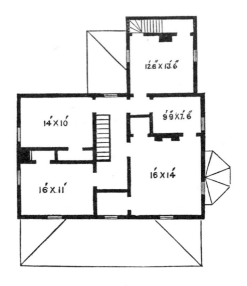

FIG. 188.—PLAN SECOND FLOOR.

dow, this house can be built in the suburbs of New
York for about $4,500. The work to be well done; the
interior finish to be plain, but the best of its class; a
hard finish white wall, neat cornices and centre-pieces
on first floor, and neatly moulded base and trimmings
throughout.

GEO. E. WOODWARD,

ARCHITECT, CIVIL & LANDSCAPE ENGINEER,

191 BROADWAY, NEW YORK.

WOODWARD'S

ARCHITECTURE

AND RURAL ART.

No. II.——1868.

BY

GEO. E. WOODWARD,

ARCHITECT AND CIVIL ENGINEER,

AUTHOR OF "WOODWARD'S COUNTRY HOMES."

NEW YORK:

GEO. E. WOODWARD, 191 BROADWAY.

1868.

Davies and Kent,
Electrotypers and Stereotypers,
183 William St., N. Y.

EDWARD O. JENKINS,
Printer & Stereotyper,
No. 20 North William St.

INTRODUCTION.

WE endeavor in each number of this annual publica-
tion to give some fresh and valuable suggestions relative
to designing and building Country Houses, and to meet,
to some extent, the improving taste for convenient and
beautiful homes.

There is a growing appreciation for improved styles
of building which is being recognized throughout all the
better settled portions of our country. More favorable
sites are chosen, and more consideration given to views
from the house and to the effect produced by the house
from all points.

In a country like this, abounding in desirable locations
with agreeable surroundings, there is ample space for
displaying good judgment in the selection of a site on
which to build and embellish a country residence.

The position of the building should be settled somewhat by the tastes of the family who are to occupy it.

Convenient access, sunny exposures, commanding views, trees, etc., are all to be considered; but the best spot on the property owned is the one to be made use of, and minor requirements to be made, as far as possible, to correspond.

In this, as in the former work, we give different combinations of plans, to suit requirements made by different tastes or necessities. But as we live in the country for room, fresh air, daylight, and sunshine, we must necessarily condemn all underground apartments. Cellar kitchens and other similar contrivances may be tolerated as a matter of economy only in the first cost; and wherever built through such necessities, the time should always be looked forward to when suitable additions can be made above ground.

In No. I. of this series a large number of designs were given for low-priced cottages, farm-houses, etc., together with numerous plans for barns and all classes of out-buildings, and designs for laying out and embellishing small plots of ground from small village lots up to ten acres in extent. This number is devoted more particularly to a class of houses contemplating a more liberal expenditure, and introducing examples of the French or Mansard roof, which is attracting attention from all; and when amount of room is considered, is as economical as any style that can be selected. It is not, however, so suitable for small cottages. To have the best effect, it should be applied to houses of liberal size and accommodation, and should be treated by one thoroughly conversant with its proportions. There is ample room for display of skill in the design of a house with this style of roof, and boldness should be a prominent characteristic.

Our plans for the future are to devote our entire attention to the subject of improving Country and Suburban Homes, and developing the beauties of the surrounding grounds; and we intend in each annual issue of this volume to demonstrate the fact, that the convenience, beauty, and elegance of a Country Home may be attained by a moderate expenditure, and thus making the desire to possess, improve, and retain permanently, become a leading trait with all. Our plans will be practical; and in addition to the resources of many years of successful professional practice in all departments of Rural Art, we shall give examples of some of the work of the best experts in the profession.

We aim to give a reliable progressive exponent of Rural Art, an invaluable aid to all who seek to have a home around which will cluster the most delightful associations.

CONTENTS.

DESIGN No. 1.

A SUBURBAN HOUSE.

BY GEO. E. HARNEY, COLD SPRING, NEW YORK.

FIG. 2.—SUBURBAN HOUSE.

THE square, or nearly square, house, with the French or Mansard roof, seems to be especially appropriate for the narrow lots in the suburbs and in larger country towns. Of late years this style has become extremely popular, and, we think, deservedly so, since it undoubtedly gives a greater amount of available room than any of the other modes, and is always in good keeping with the somewhat formal surroundings in a thickly settled neighborhood.

From the peculiar construction of the roof, the attics of such houses may contain as many, and nearly as good, chambers as the second floor, and, on that account, a house requiring a certain amount of accommodation may be smaller than if it were in any of the other styles.

The plan, too, providing a hall in the middle with rooms on

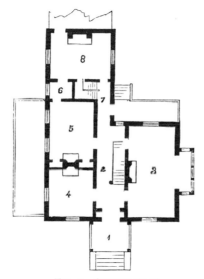

Fig. 3.—Ground Plan.

either side, has always been a favorite, particularly with practical, matter-of-fact people, who like to see every inch accounted for, and who have a horror of twists and turns and out-of-the-way corners.

In the design here given will be found accommodation for quite a large family, with considerable economy of space, united, we think, to a respectable appearance of exterior. The house is supposed to be situated on the corner of the street, the entrance portico being on one front and a large bay window on the other.

The entrance hall, containing the staircase, is eight feet wide; it opens into the parlor on the right hand, and into the library and dining-room on the left; and, at the extreme end into another hall containing the private stairways, to the cellar and the chambers.

The parlor is sixteen feet by twenty-four, exclusive of a roomy bay window opening from its longest side, and overlooking the street.

The library is sixteen feet square, and the dining-room sixteen feet by eighteen. Connecting the dining-room and kitchen is a large pantry fitted up with shelves and cupboards, and other conveniences usually found in such places.

The kitchen is sixteen feet by eighteen, and is provided with a range, hot and cold water fixtures complete, dressers, etc., and has attached a pantry or sink-room, through which we pass to the yard.

The basement contains a laundry, two large store-rooms, and an open cellar with a cemented floor and a plastered ceiling. There are also provided a furnace, coal-bins, ash-box, wine-closet, etc., etc.

The second floor contains four chambers in the main body of the house, two of which have large dressing-rooms attached, and two smaller chambers in the kitchen wing, besides a bathing-room and several closets.

The attic has four chambers, each of which is provided with a large closet, and another room which may be used as a store-room.

The ceilings measure ten and a half, ten, and nine feet high in the several stories.

DESIGN No. 2.

A COUNTRY HOUSE.

FIG. 4.—COUNTRY HOUSE—PERSPECTIVE VIEW.

THE design of this house was made for the purpose of giving each room a sunny southern exposure, and out of ten rooms nine have at least one look-out to the southeast, and one, the small room over the hall, has a southwest window. There is a fine cellar under the whole house, the rear of which can be finished for a laundry, and has an outside cellar door.

The principal floor is so managed that the spacious hall with winding staircase presents an attractive feature on entering. The chimney is in the center of the house, and sliding doors connect each of the principal rooms, so that, when occasion requires, hall, parlor, library, and dining-room may be thrown together, the octagon form of these rooms adding much to their

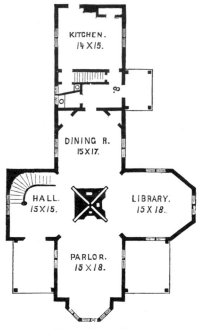

FIG. 5.—FIRST FLOOR.

beauty. Back of the dining-room is a side hall, closets, side door, and back stairway, and back of these the kitchen, provided with sink and force pump, connecting with a thoroughly constructed cistern of 8,000 gallons capacity, which receives all the water from a slate roof. Rain water from a slate roof is pure and clean, free from color, and used with ice in summer is better and healthier than well water.

The kitchen is well ventilated, windows both sides, and doors so arranged as to secure comfort ; an independent chimney, etc.

The second floor has large and well-ventilated bedrooms, ceilings are square and of good height, abundant closet room, etc.

Above this, in the tower, is a fine octagon room of fifteen feet radius, that can be used for a bedroom, smoking-room, or any other purpose; a good garret, also, for storage, etc.

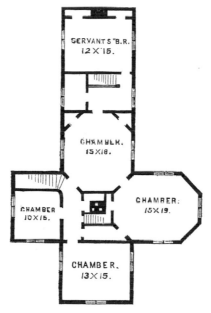

FIG. 6.—SECOND FLOOR.

The house to be heated with a furnace. In the parlor and library are marble mantles, and each is fitted with Dixon's low-down Philadelphia polished steel grates for burning wood or coal —the best open fire known.

The frame is substantial, and lined throughout with unworked lumber, and covered with narrow-lapped siding, making a stiff, warm house.

FIG. 7.—A SIMPLE RUSTIC COTTAGE.

DESIGN No. 3.

A RUSTIC COTTAGE.

BY G. E. HARNEY, COLD SPRING, N. Y.

THIS design represents a simple rustic cottage for a family of small means. It is built of wood, filled in with soft brick on edge, and covered in the vertical and battened manner, with rough boards and heavy battens, care being taken in laying the boards on, that the splinters of the wood made by the saw in sawing from the log point downward instead of upward, to shed the water more effectually. The roof is covered with shingles, and the projections of the gables, which are quite heavy, are relieved by ornamental verge boards sawn from heavy plank. The windows have all bold trimmings, and those on the lower story are protected by broad hoods, and glazed with diamond-shaped glass. The veranda, or front stoop, is made with cedar posts and trimmings, but has a plank floor and tight roof. The chimneys represented are terra-cotta chimney tops of large size, resting upon a blue-stone base cut for the purpose.

The interior arrangement is as follows: The hall, No. 1, measures eight feet by eleven, and contains stairs to the chamber and cellar. The principal stairs are three feet wide, and the cellar flight is two feet eight inches, inclosed by a partition with a door at the top. No. 2 is the living-room, fourteen feet square, provided with an open fire-place for burning wood, and also having on one of its sides a recess or bay, with side lights only, the back being made to serve the purpose of a book-case or cupboard. No. 3 is the kitchen, twelve by fourteen, well lighted by two large windows, and having a large closet opening out of the side beyond the fire-place. No. 4 is a pantry, measuring five by eight, and opening out upon the back stoop. This pantry may have a sink in it, and may be fitted up with shelves and cupboards. Additional room may be got by putting the kitchen in the basement, and using the upper room as a living or dining room, and the front room as a parlor. This would give an opportunity for finishing the parlor in a little more expensive manner, and on that account may be more desirable.

Fig. 8.—Interior Arrangement.

The second floor contains two good-sized chambers and four large closets. There is no attic to the house, but a space of about five feet in height is left above the chamber and below the peak of the roof, which serves a good purpose as ventilator.

The posts are fourteen feet high, and the lower story is finished nine feet high in the clear. The finish of the interior is all of pine, and put up in a simple manner. The walls are all plastered, and finished with a rough white sand finish, which may afterward be tinted in any desirable shade. The outside should be painted two or three tints.

DESIGN No. 4.

A VILLAGE RESIDENCE.

BY ROBERT MOOK, ARCHITECT, 111 BROADWAY, NEW YORK.

Fig. 9.—Village Residence.

We show here a design for a medium-sized cottage, such as one might build on a village lot of sixty or a hundred feet in width.

It is a framed building, filled in with brick (soft brick might be used), laid on their edges in mortar, and covered externally with weather-boarding; the roof covered with shingles cut in patterns.

The framing may be of spruce or hemlock timber (the former is the best, but the latter is generally used), and the finishing of white pine; the details few, simple, and bold, with the roof quite steep, and the eaves of broad projection, to shield the sides, and the windows wide and airy. A light ridge ornament at the peak of the roof, a finial of iron over the dormer, and the piazza railing of scroll-sawed penetrations, give a character to the design.

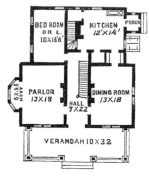
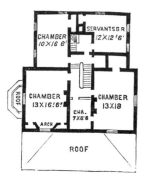

Fig. 10.—First Floor.   Fig. 11.—Second Floor.

The accommodation of the plan is as follows: A veranda, 10 feet wide, shields the front of the first story, from which leads a hall 7 feet wide, and containing the stairway to the chamber floor; a parlor, 13 feet by 18 feet, on the left of the hall, with a bay window opposite the door, with a library or chamber back of it; on the right hand of the hall is a dining-room, 13 feet by 18 feet, communicating with the kitchen, situated back of the dining-room, with closets and passage-way between; behind the kitchen fire-place is placed the private stairway to the chamber floor, and under the same the stairway to the cellar.

A porch covers the back door leading from the kitchen, which may be inclosed, and be used as a scullery.

The chamber floor contains five chambers, of large, medium, and smaller size, with closets to each ; and in the back part of the hall are inclosed stairs leading to the garret, which is here meant to be left unfinished but is capable of containing several good rooms.

The cellar is to be under the whole of the house, affording ample room for all sorts of storage, cold-room, store-room, bins, etc.

It is not intended in this design to introduce any superfluous fittings ; the closets fitted simply with shelves and hooks ; the wood-work white, or (which is better) to be grained or tinted with color ; and the walls of the principal rooms may be enriched with some simple, tasty paper-hangings. The hall floor may be laid with alternate strips of walnut and ash, which costs but little more than good oil-cloth, and does not need renewing.

The exterior should be painted of a warm rich brown, or yellowish brown, using four tints, the lightest for the whole body of the house ; the next darkest for the eaves, veranda, window trimmings, etc. ; the third darkest for window-sashes, blinds, etc. ; and the darkest only for touching up here and there, to make it appear lively.

DESIGN No. 5.

A   C O T T A G E.

BY GEORGE E. HARNEY, COLD SPRING, N. Y.

FIG. 12.—A COTTAGE.

THE plan of this house has been adopted, in a number of instances, where cheapness and compactness of accommodation
were particularly desirable; and in each instance there has been
made some considerable alteration in the exterior, to suit the
fancies of different parties or the requirements of different locations.   In the design before us, the principal feature of the exterior is the covered balcony over the entrance porch, which by

its depth of shadow gives boldness to the front and adds much to the convenience of the plan, opening as it does out of the two principal chambers of the house, and affording comfort and retirement to the occupants. In winter, it may be shut in by a glass front, and will form then a very pleasant little conservatory—a luxury which houses of this size seldom afford.

The front door is shielded by a broad hood, and the stoop has seats protected by a railing at the sides.

The front entry, No. 1, is 5 feet by 9, and opens into the living-room, No. 2, 12 feet by 17; this opens into a pantry, No. 3

Fig. 13.—Ground Plan.

which is fitted up with sink, cupboard, shelves, and other conveniences. No. 4 is the parlor, 12 feet square; and No. 6 is a large closet or pantry, opening out of the parlor, and fitted up with shelves and drawers.

The cellar stairs descend from the pantry, and the cellar has coal and wood bins and hanging shelves, etc. In the second story are three chambers, one over the parlor, and two smaller ones over the living-room. Each has a closet attached, and the two front ones open upon the balcony before mentioned by means of French casement windows.

In one of the designs to which this plan was adapted, an extra chamber was made in the place of the covered balcony, and the exterior was finished otherwise in a more ornamental manner. The second story projected over the first about ten inches, and was finished in the vertical and battened manner, the boards being all reduced to a uniform width, and the lower ends, which projected over, were sawn in an ornamental drop pattern.

The principal story exterior was covered with shingles, also cut to a pattern, and nailed to hemlock boarding.

In another design, the gables were all cut off, and the roofs, which were much flatter, projected three feet all around, and were supported on heavy brackets--somewhat after the manner of Swiss houses—the front and rear projections being continuations of the main roof.

The house in each instance was built of wood, filled in with brick, and the roofs covered with slate.

Both stories measured 9 feet high in the clear, and all the rooms had open fire-places. The walls were hard finished throughout, and all the inside wood-work was stained a dark color and varnished.

The floors, which were laid with narrow plank in courses, were stained alternately light and dark.

The exteriors were painted with grays and drabs, varied in shade and tint.

This design, which was the simplest of them all, cost, in 1864, about $1,500.

DESIGN No. 6.

A DWELLING-HOUSE—ITALIAN STYLE.

FIG. 14.—DWELLING-HOUSE ITALIAN STYLE PERSPECTIVE VIEW.

THIS design was made for erection in Rutherfurd Park, N. J., and is a good example of a compact, convenient, and economical country house with good commodious rooms, well connected, and easily heated and ventilated. The basement contains besides the necessary cellar and coal requisites, a fine billiard-room; and as a solid substantial foundation is thus secured, it is perhaps the best part of the house for such a purpose, occupying room not needed otherwise, and not objectionable to the most fastidious.   The parlor and dining-room connect with each other, and each has independent communication with a spacious hall or vestibule, and this latter it is proposed to fit up in an imposing manner. The stairway is of easy rise and tread, with rail and newel of attractive proportions; the ceilings to be groined, walls paneled,

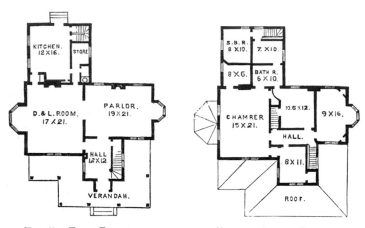

FIG. 15.—FIRST FLOOR.   FIG. 16.—SECOND FLOOR.

etc.; the full arrangement of bedrooms, closets, etc., is easily seen from the plans; no space is lost—all room is made available.

The construction of the house is of wood, balloon frame, diagonally boarded outside with unworked plank, then covered with roofing felt, and weather-boarded with narrow lap-siding.   The work throughout to be well done, finish substantial and plain, walls hard finish, tin roof, etc.

The location of this house is such that every room commands extensive river, mountain, and inland views, and from the upper tower room is seen the whole valley of the Lower Passaic, with its fruitful farms and princely country seats, and the distant spires of its two flourishing cities, Paterson and Newark.

Rutherfurd Park is a magnificent estate of upward of 300 acres of handsome rolling land, superbly wooded and watered, and rising from the river bank to an elevation of one hundred feet above tide water. It lies three quarters of a mile from the Boiling Spring Depot, Erie Railway, and is reached by a broad and magnificent boulevard running through the entire property. An expenditure of $10,000 makes this one of the finest drives in the country. As a home for New York business men who enjoy

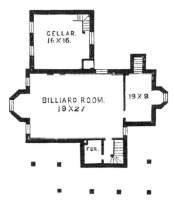

Fig. 17.—Cellar Plan.

country life; who wish to reside within a moderate distance of their business, and reach it with absolute certainty from daylight to midnight; who can not afford either the time, the expense, or the annoyance of living above Thirty-eighth Street; who prefer to ride in broad-guage palaces instead of filthy horse cars, Rutherfurd Park and its surroundings present attractions of the most decided and fascinating character.

FIG. 18.—A SUBURBAN RESIDENCE.

DESIGN No. 7.

A SUBURBAN RESIDENCE.

BY CARL PFEIFFER, ARCHITECT, 4 BROAD STREET, NEW YORK.

THE accompanying design is one of twelve houses built on Staten Island about three years ago. It is of brick, with brown stone trimmings, and faced with Philadelphia front brick, and

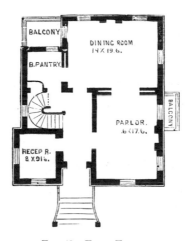

FIG. 19.—FIRST FLOOR.

has a slate roof. Having fine views in all directions, it was thought more desirable to have the kitchen, laundry, and servants' rooms in the basement; but should it be preferred to have

FIG. 20.—A SUBURBAN RESIDENCE, SHOWING MANSARD ROOF TO TOWER.

the kitchen on a level with the ground floor, a wing could be added, as indicated by fig. 23. For reasons of economy, the Mansard roof of the tower was omitted; what the effect of it would be, can be seen by referring to the perspective fig. 20. The ground floor contains a reception-room or library, parlor, dining-room, butler's pantry, and hall closets. In the principal front to the right of the tower, it will be seen that the rectangular form of the lower story was not continued in the second, but

FIG. 21.—SECOND FLOOR.

gives a semi-octagon appearance to the second story front, affording a balcony at one angle and a convenient entrance to an oriel window at the other angle.

This oriel window has proved a desirable feature, especially to the ladies of the house, to read. to write, or sew in, affording a fine view in several directions; it also forms a pleasing feature of the exterior.

The house was built by days' work, but it is estimated to cost $8,000.

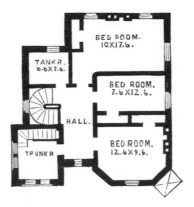

FIG. 22.—THIRD FLOOR.

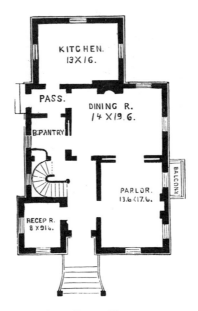

FIG. 23.—FIRST FLOOR, KITCHEN CONNECTED.

DESIGN No. 8.

A VILLA.

BY G. E. HARNEY, ARCHITECT, COLD SPRING, N. Y.

FIG. 24.—A VILLA.

THIS design was built about two years ago, and is now owned and occupied by P. K. Paulding, Esq., of Cold Spring, N. Y.

It is built of wood, filled in with brick, and roofed with slate. It has a fine cellar underneath, containing laundry, store-rooms, wine-room, and coal and wood bins; is warmed throughout by one of Boynton's base burning furnaces, having in addition open fire-places for wood in every room; is supplied with range and plumbing, with hot and cold water in the bathing-room; and contains in all fifteen rooms, as follows:

Nos. 1 and 2—The hall, extending through the building from front to rear, and opening, at the farther end, by French windows, upon a wide veranda which commands an extensive view of the Hudson River and the surrounding mountains.

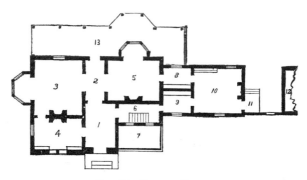

FIG. 25.—GROUND PLAN.

No. 3—Parlor, sixteen feet by eighteen, exclusive of the bay window which was more recently built, and which adds much to the appearance and convenience of the room.

No. 4—Library, twelve by sixteen, surrounded by fixed bookcases, and communicating with the parlor and the front hall.

No. 5—Dining-room, fifteen by sixteen, exclusive of a bay window which projects about five feet from the room, and around which the western veranda extends.

No. 6—A staircase hall, containing stairs to the chambers and to the cellar—shut off from the main hall by a door, and having easy communication with the kitchen.

No. 7—A gallery or terrace, opening from the entrance hall by French windows.

No. 8—A butler's pantry, connecting the kitchen with the dining-room, and fitted up with cupboards, etc.

No. 10—The kitchen, fifteen feet square—opening out into the yard by a stoop, No. 11.

No. 12—A small wood-shed for storing wood, etc. It was found, after the house had been occupied for some time, that the kitchen accommodation was somewhat limited, and, quite recently, the small building before used as a wood-shed has been joined to the kitchen wing, and now serves the purpose of an outer kitchen and servants' hall. Connecting with it is another building, recently added, which is used as a wood and coal shed, etc.

The second floor contains four good-sized chambers in the main portion, and a bathing-room, a large dressing-room, and a large wardrobe in the kitchen wing, besides a good number of closets. The attic has three chambers, and a large open space for trunks, etc.

An important feature of the house is a large ventilator on the peak of the roof—having sashes in its four sides which can be opened or shut at pleasure by means of ropes and pulleys. When any or all the sashes are opened, a thorough circulation of air is produced in all parts of the house ; and in summer particularly—even during the hottest weather, when the doors and windows of the lower stories were kept open — an agreeable current was maintained at all times.

The first story is ten feet high, and the second nine feet.

The wood-work throughout—with the exception of the parlor, which is painted in tints—is stained light, with dark moldings, and the walls of all the rooms of the lower story are painted in oil in different tints.

DESIGN No. 9.

A SEA-SIDE COTTAGE.

BY F. S. COPLEY, ARTIST, TOMPKINSVILLE, N. Y.

FIG. 26.—A SEA-SIDE COTTAGE—PERSPECTIVE VIEW.

THIS cottage was intended for a summer resort on the sea-side, for a small family keeping but one servant. It will be seen to combine with a picturesque exterior convenience of arrangement and economy of construction.

It was intended to be built of wood (balloon framed), filled in with brick, and roofed with shingles cut in patterns, and finished throughout in a plain cottage-like but substantial manner—the posts, rail, etc., of the veranda to be formed of the trunks and branches of the red cedar tree, left rough, with the bark on.

The accommodation consists of seven good rooms, a cellar, and all other necessary conveniences, and are arranged as follows. (See fig. 27, principal plan.)

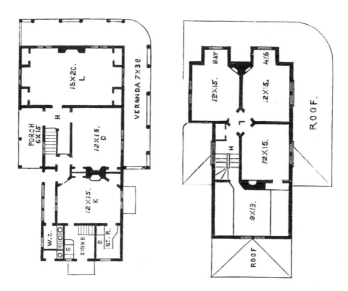

FIG. 27.—FIRST FLOOR.   FIG. 28.—SECOND FLOOR.

H, the hall, entered from the porch by double doors, with swinging sash panels, which pleasantly light and ventilate it. On the left, as you enter, is the living-room, lighted by four windows, each commanding fine views of the sea and surrounding country. The one in front is finished with a seat; the other three are French casements, opening to the floor, to give access to the veranda. Four closets for books, etc., are so arranged at the ends of the room as to give the pretty effect of bay windows. The fire-place is made for burning wood on the hearth, in the old style. This is quite a large and handsome apartment for so small a cottage. being twenty by fifteen feet, and ten feet high.

The door opposite the entrance leads into a cheerful little dining-room, possessing the same fine view of the sea from its casement window, and access to the veranda, as the parlor. Closets for glass and china (with a pass in the latter) are fitted up on each side of the fire-place. By this is a door to the lobby, which communicates with the hall, kitchen, hat and cloak closet (under the stairs), and outside, etc. The outer door is lighted in the panel and protected by a rustic veranda, intended to be covered with vines.

The kitchen is well lighted, and arranged for the especial convenience of the housekeeper, with everything needful at hand—closets, dresser, and range (with hot and cold water), store-room, and scullery (with sink, water, and fuel in an adjoining lean-to). The cellar is under the kitchen, and entered from the scullery—there is no leaving shelter for anything.

Ascending the stairs to the second story (see fig. 28, chamber plan), on the landing to the right is the servant's room, thirteen feet by nine, made in the roof of the wing over the kitchen. This room is well lighted in the gable, and ventilated by a valve in the chimney, like all the rest, and has large stow-away rubbish closets on each side. A few steps more to the left is the upper hall, lighted by the front dormer, and fitted with a clothes-press and linen-closet. By this is a small lobby, with sky-light and ventilator above, communicating with three light and airy family chambers, each fifteen feet by twelve, and nine feet high, with closets, fire-places, etc.

DESIGN No. 10.

REMODELING AN OLD HOUSE.

BY G. E. HARNEY, COLD SPRING, N. Y.

FIG. 29.—THE OLD HOUSE.

THE accompanying sketches will convey a good idea of some alterations and additions made to an old house in this neighborhood, under our direction.

Though it is always an exceedingly interesting task, it is not always a very easy one, to make a new and comely house out of an old and ugly one; there are so many stubborn points to contend with—so much has to be undone before anything satisfactory can be done, and this was no exception to the rule. The house was very small, very ugly, and situated very close to the

FIG. 30.—THE OLD HOUSE REMODELED.

sidewalk; but the walls were in good condition, the foundations were solid, the partitions were right, and, for other good reasons, it was not deemed desirable to destroy it. Accordingly the work of remodeling was undertaken.

The results, which we here give, we have reason to believe to be quite satisfactory, and we place them before the reader as an answer to a number of inquiries which have lately been made of us on this subject.

The house, at the time of its purchase by the present proprietor, was a plain, two-story brick building, measuring twenty-two feet by twenty-four, with a narrow veranda extending along the front, and close to the sidewalk, as represented in fig. 29.

It had a hall five and a half feet wide, extending through from front to rear, with a door at each end, and in this hall was the staircase, which occupied so much space that there was barely room to pass around it. On the right was a room about fifteen feet square, and directly back of that were two other rooms, formerly used, we presume, as bedrooms, each about seven feet square. The kitchen was in the basement, and there were three chambers on the second floor. (The original plan is shown by the darker lines in the engraving.)

The alterations were somewhat as follows: In order to throw the front as far away from the street as possible, the veranda was taken entirely away and its place supplied by a narrow balcony, opening from the rooms by French windows.

To carry out this idea still further, the entrance was recessed about three feet, so that the front doors were about thirteen feet from the fence.

The staircases were taken away and new ones put up, farther back, taking up the space before occupied by one of the little bedrooms, so that the hall was left free and clear of obstructions. These stairways were made winding, and the hall, extending through both the principal stories and the attic, was surmounted by a large skylight and ventilator, the whole height being about twenty-six feet.

The old roof was taken off and the walls carried up about three feet higher, in order to get a large servants' room in the old part; and as the rooms of the old part were lower than was desirable in the new, the three tiers of rooms there made up a height equal to the two stories of the addition. A hipped roof, with a bracketed cornice, then covered the whole building.

Six rooms were added, three on each floor (see the lighter portions of the plan), and the whole accommodation of the house as it now stands is as follows:

1. The front door recess, opening into No. 2, the hall, which, with No. 3, the sitting-room, and a portion of the pantry, No. 7, make up the whole of the original house.

FIG. 31.—GROUND PLAN.

No. 4. Parlor, sixteen feet by twenty, connected by folding doors with the library, No. 5, ten feet by sixteen, which, in its turn, opens, by folding doors, into No. 6, the dining-room, a pleasant apartment, sixteen feet by twenty. This dining-room also opens directly into the main hall, at the foot of the stair-case. The parlor has a large French window in the front, opening directly out upon the veranda, No. 9, seen also in the engraving, fig. 30, and both library and dining-room open out upon a gallery, No. 8, which extends along the rear of the house.

The library is fitted up with stationary low bookcases, and all the rooms have open fire-places.

The pantry, No. 7, is seven feet wide by about fifteen feet long, and has shelves and cupboards for china, etc., a large dumb-waiter from the kitchen, and a wash bowl with hot and cold water fixtures. The stairs to the kitchen are under the main flight, and are shut off from the principal hall. The kitchen occupies all of the basement of the old house except that portion taken up by the staircase, and is unusually large and complete in its arrangements for a house of this extent. It is about twenty feet wide and twenty-two feet long; it has one of Quimby's large ranges, with all the fixtures complete, including a sixty-gallon copper boiler and plumbing arrangements; a cast-iron sink, with slab and dripping boards; a dresser occupying the whole of one side; and, in a closet, a dumb-waiter rising to the pantry above.

Under the dining-room is a laundry, fitted up with three stationary wash trays and a cast-iron wash sink; and under the parlor and library is the open cellar, which has a cemented floor and a plastered ceiling; two coal-bins and a wine-closet are here provided. In the chamber story there are four chambers, three of which have large closets, and the fourth a dressing-room attached. There is a bath-room on this floor, directly over the pantry.

The attic provides servants' rooms and an open garret.

Gas and hot and cold water are provided throughout, and the house is very satisfactorily heated by a furnace. The finish is plain throughout, but the workmanship is of good quality; the walls are all finished rough, and are tinted in a variety of shades, suited to the different uses of the rooms.

FIG. 32.—FRENCH OR MANSARD ROOFED HOUSE.

DESIGN No. 11.

FRENCH OR MANSARD ROOFED HOUSE.

WE show, in this design, a very compact, roomy, sensible house, possessing a great deal of comfort, and not profuse in ornament or show. It is such a house as one might live in and enjoy this life to a full reasonable extent. The Mansard roof gives great abundance of chamber room, and as it should be of good height, with air space above, these rooms may be quite as comfortable as any in the house.

The deck or upper roof is tinned, after having been carefully covered with one-and-a-quarter-inch pine floor plank, which, if expense is not closely considered, would be better of narrow width, and laid smoothly and carefully. The gutter inside the cornice of deck roof can convey water to a tank on the third floor. All tin roofing and workmanship should be of the best class, thoroughly painted and protected from the weather. The lower or steep portion of the Mansard roof should be boarded in the same manner as for the tin. Over this place roofing felt (tarred paper), and then lay the slate. The smaller sizes cut to some of the numerous patterns and laid with an alternate band of some distinct color would give a pretty effect. The main cornice gutter should be spacious; the too prevailing fault with all gutters is their lack of capacity in heavy driving storms.

A house of this size and style looks well, built of almost any good material; with brick or stone would present an effective appearance, and impress one with a substantial and comfortable air. In building a house of this class, although of moderate dimensions, it would be good policy to build well. Good, well-built houses, free from extravagant finish and ornament, always represent the money they cost, and are usually the most satisfactory to own and occupy.

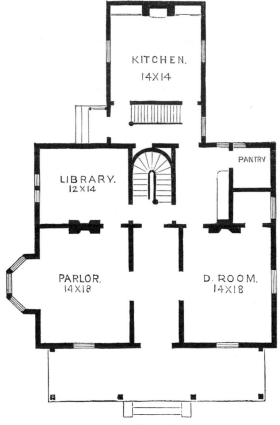

FIG. 33.—FIRST FLOOR.

In connection herewith we specify the leading points and materials in the construction, briefly hinting in such a manner as will convey to the mind of a good mechanic or contractor the class of materials and workmanship required. Specifications are for the purpose of informing the builder on all those points that can not be expressed in the drawing, such as quality of

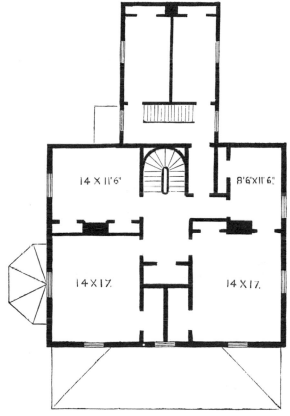

FIG. 34.—SECOND FLOOR.

materials, manner of putting them together, etc.; but they are never intended, as some suppose, to teach a workman his trade. A builder of experience, and in fact any one of good sense, comprehends more easily short, compact instructions.

Voluminous specifications may be required for the purpose of holding a contractor on every point, and, if this were possible, to make men honest, no one could object. But it will not answer this purpose. He who lets a contract to irresponsible men, or to those who live by evading the spirit and intent,

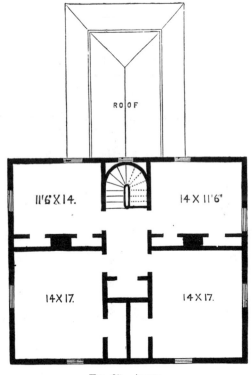

FIG. 35.—ATTIC.

merely because their price is smaller, deserves to suffer. Contractors, like all other men, follow their business for a livelihood; they do their business at the market price because they are in pursuit of business to do. They take contracts for the express purpose of making money out of them. The man of capital and reputation requires his price, and in the end is the cheapest. He calculates to finish his work, and to finish it well; to do all he agreed to do, and perhaps more; and in letting a contract, reputation and ability should have its full influence. It won't pay to experiment with weak men at a low price. A man with a small purse should have as good a price for work as one of large means.

There will be, however, a considerable difference in the proposals of responsible contractors, and this may arise from several causes, such as surplus of work, distance from site, and the different facilities different men have for executing work.

The following style of specification we have found, in practice, to answer the best purpose. It is short and comprehensive, but it will fail, as indeed will all others, to tie up any mechanic or contractor who does business in any manner that is unfair or objectionable. In making use of them, or adapting them to other buildings, it will be necessary to supply such other instructions as may be required. It is not complete on all headings for all buildings, or for all classes of work.

SPECIFICATIONS FOR PROVIDING MATERIALS AND LABOR FOR THE CONSTRUCTION OF A DWELLING-HOUSE.

EXCAVATION.

CELLAR.—To be excavated to the depth of four and a half feet from average level. Surface soil kept separate.

CISTERN.—To be excavated twelve feet in diameter, and twelve feet deep.

VAULT.—Privy vault to be eight by ten feet, and six feet deep.

DITCHES, CESSPOOL.—Ditches for drainage from house to be
dug; also for overflow and supply pipes for cistern.
When pipes are laid, the same to be filled up.   Make
excavation for cesspool, piers, steps, and for all purposes
required.

WELL.—To be dug or bored, as directed by owner, stoned up or
tubed; provided with hoisting apparatus, and made complete for use.   Design for well-house to be furnished.
Earth taken from well to be placed where directed.

GRADING.—After mason work for above is finished, the earth to
be graded or removed, and, as far as possible, the surface
soil to be placed on top.

MASON WORK.

CELLAR WALLS.—Cellar walls to be twenty inches in thickness,
to start six inches below cellar bottom, on broad footing
stones, and to be built six and a half feet above cellar
bottom.   Stone to be of suitable quality for good rubble
masonry, to be laid in best mortar, thoroughly bonded
and joints suitably pointed.   Walls above ground to be
pointed outside; put in all areas, coal-slides, cellar-doors,
and do all masonry required on plan.   Cellar windows to
have stone sills, and outside cellar-steps to be of stone.
Piers for veranda to be built of brick, and flag-stones two
and a half by four feet provided for each outside door.
Coal-slide to have flag-stone bottom and top, and to be
provided with chain and cover set in flag-stone in usual
manner.

CHIMNEYS to be placed as shown; foundations to start from
cellar bottom; all to be of best hard brick laid in mortar.   One flue in each chimney to start from cellar, and
one flue from each room through which the chimneys

pass; fire-places to be built where shown, and of the size indicated with arch for hearth; where no fire-place is shown, provide place for stove-pipe, and six-inch registers for ventilation. Top out chimneys per plan, and lay the upper courses in cement; all chimneys to be flashed with tin; ash-pits to be built for Dixon grates where shown; all flues to be smoothly pargeted, and where drawn or twisted, to be done without injury to draft. Kitchen fire-place to have large stone hearth and mantel.

FURNACE, RANGE, AND MANTELS.—Do all mason work and furnish all materials necessary to set furnace and range in a complete and workman-like manner. Furnace to set on flag-stone of suitable size. Provide and set all mantels, as shown on plan, and set all grates required; mantels and grates to be approved of by owner.

CISTERN.—To be built of best hard brick, circular form, eight-inch wall, laid in cement, bottom to be grouted in usual manner; top to be covered with flat arch, built of brick, eight inches thick, laid in the best manner with cement, finished two feet below final surface of ground, and provided with man-hole two feet in diameter. Also, supply and overflow vitrified pipes of suitable size to be built in. The whole interior of the cistern to be covered with two coats of best cement, and made tight and serviceable; the top of arch to have two coats of cement before being covered with earth; man-hole to be inclosed with eight-inch brick wall, cemented outside and in, carried up to surface, and provided with suitable stone cover with iron ring; cistern to be ten feet deep and ten feet in diameter.

PRIVY VAULT.—To be built of stone, laid dry, top course above ground to be laid in mortar.

DRAINAGE.—Provide and lay one drain from house of vitrified
pipe six inches in diameter, one hundred feet long, with
trap, and build cesspool for discharge; provide and lay
three-inch vitrified pipe from leaders to cistern, and for
surplus water from roofs provide and lay three-inch vitrified pipe from leaders to main drain, and provide all
elbows, angles, and tees required for all connections; lay
a suitable-sized vitrified pipe from cistern for overflow.

LATHING AND PLASTERING.—All interior walls and ceilings,
cellar and garret excepted, to be lathed and plastered;
two coats best mortar suitably mixed, laid and floated, of
best materials and workmanship, and finished in the
best manner with hard-finish white coat; neat cornices
to be run on first-floor ceilings, in hall, and principal
rooms, and two neat and approved center-pieces to be
provided and set.

GROUTING.—The cellar floor to be grouted and cemented in the
best manner.

The first floor to be deafened throughout, by grouting
between the beams, in the usual manner, and made
rat-proof.

FINALLY—Provide all materials and workmanship necessary to
fully complete for occupation, and to comply with the
intent and meaning of plans and specifications—the
whole to be approved of by the owner or his superin-
tendent.

CARPENTER WORK.

FRAME.—Building to be framed in the style known as "Balloon
Frame." Studs, floor beams, and rafters to be placed
16 inches apart.

Sills, 3 by 8, halved at angles and joints.

Corner posts, 4 by 6.

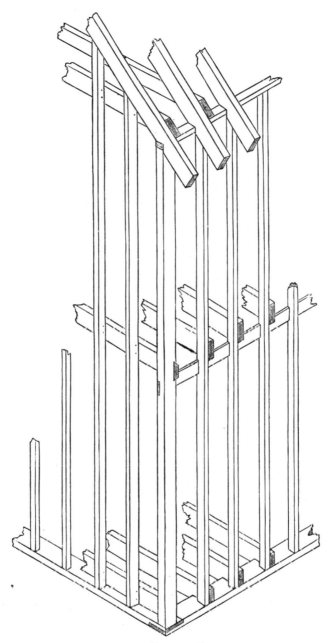

FIG. 35.—BALLOON FRAME.

Studding,   2 by 4.
Door and Window studs, 3 by 4.
Side girts,   1 by 6, gained in.
Plates,   3 by 4.
Floor beams,   3 by 8, well bridged.
Rafters,   3 by 6.
Timber, spruce; and the frame to be securely nailed.
French roof, to be framed in usual manner.

OUTSIDE BOARDING AND WEATHER-BOARDING.—The outside of
frame to be boarded with worked and matched pine
boards, well nailed, then to be covered with roofing felt
or tarred paper, and weather-boarded with narrow dressed lap siding.

FLOORING.—To be narrow 1¼ in., worked and matched floor
plank, blind nailed, and smoothly dressed after laying.
Garret floor to be laid with wide pine boards, dressed.

ROOFING.—All roofs to be covered with worked and matched
pine boards; the deck and veranda roofs to be covered
with best quality of tin; the lower Mansard roof to be
slated over roofing felt, in fancy patterns and colors.

GUTTERS, VALLEYS, LEADERS.—Gutters to be made wherever
necessary, to convey all the water from all roofs, either to
cistern or drain; valleys to be thoroughly tinned, and
leaders of suitable size to be provided, put up, and connected with pipes to cistern or drain.

All flat roofs to be tinned with best quality roofing tin;
and all tin work to be thoroughly painted with two coats
of paint suitable for the purpose.

HOT AIR TUBES FOR FURNACE.—Hot air tubes and registers
to be provided by tinner, put up, and connected with
furnace.

WINDOWS.—To be of the size shown; all sash to be hung with weights, and provided with fastenings; sash to be one and a half inches thick, and glazed with best quality French glass.

Front door to be glazed, as shown, with French glass. Bay and parlor windows to be panneled to floor; all others finished on sills.

OUTSIDE BLINDS.—Blinds to be one and a half inches thick, rolling slats, with strong hangings and fastenings, and to be provided for all windows.

DOORS—Throughout will be four-panneled, one and three quarter inches thick, and finished alike on both sides, to be well seasoned, made of best stuff, and smoothly finished for staining.

HARDWARE.—To be of good serviceable quality; white porcelain knobs, mortice locks, etc., extra lock and trimmings for front door. All closet doors to have locks, and an ample supply of wardrobe hooks to be provided.

BASEBOARDS—Will be about seven inches in height, and of pattern suitable, one and a quarter inches thick, clear stuff, and smoothly finished. Kitchen will be wainscoted three and a half feet high.

CASINGS—From five to six inches wide, clear stuff, smoothly finished and set on base blocks.

Kitchen trimmings will be plainer.

CLOSETS.—To be shelved throughout, and amply provided with wardrobe hooks.

STAIRCASE.—To be of easy rise and tread, and provided with black walnut rail, newel and balusters of suitable pattern.

VERANDAS, BAY WINDOWS, ETC.—To be finished as shown; veranda plank to be laid in white lead; narrow one-and-a-quarter-inch plank. Posts, brackets, and trimmings per drawings.

SINK AND PUMP FOR KITCHEN.—Provide a good cast-iron sink, of suitable size, and inclose it with door, etc. Also, provide a good suction pump, cast iron, and do the necessary plumbing to connect pump with cistern, and waste-pipe from sink with drain.

FURNACE.—Furnace of suitable size to be provided, selection to be made by owner.

RANGE—To be provided for kitchen, family size, to be approved of by owner.

BELLS—From all bed-rooms on second floor, from parlor, dining-room, and front door, to be provided and hung in kitchen.

PRIVY OUTSIDE.—To be built with two apartments; outside measurement to be eight by ten feet, trimmed and plastered.

STAINING AND VARNISHING.—All interior wood-work except kitchen to be stained black walnut or satin wood, as directed, and varnished two coats, with best varnish. Puttying to be done with putty of same color as stain.

PAINTING.—All wood-work in kitchen to be painted two coats, with such tints as directed.

All outside wood-work to be painted two coats, best white lead and oil, and such tints as directed. Knots to be covered with shellac, and if loose or imperfect to be bored out and plugged.

FINALLY—Do all that is necessary to provide materials and labor to fully complete in a workman-like manner, according to plans and specifications, to the full intent and meaning thereof, and satisfactory to owner or his agent.

TO CURE SMOKY CHIMNEYS.

A FRIEND sends us the following: Place on the top a sheet-iron fixture as large as the flue, expanding as it rises, in the proportion of three at the bottom, four at the top, and fifteen high (say twelve inches bottom, sixteen inches top, and five feet high), and if the flue be about twelve inches, cut out triangles six inches deep and three inches wide at the top, forming a crown of saw-teeth.

These proportions were given to me in 1837, by Mr. Oldham, the engineer in charge of the mechanical department of the Bank of England, when he called my attention to the draught of the flues in the press-room, and then to the fixture on a neighboring chimney, and said that these rooms were almost uninhabitable when he came there, until he applied the same fixtures that he had previously used on the Bank of Ireland, and that had cost that bank about fifteen hundred pounds in experiments.

But if the top of the chimney be not above all neighboring objects, then take the same proportions in a curve, and place the adjutage on a swivel. This was done about 1842, on the flue of the House of Representatives, at Washington. The difficulty there arose from the dome. The cure was complete, as long as the experiment was tried. But in a short time a patentee obtained a contract for several flues, and his arrangement was substituted.

Again: a well-known patentee of cooking-stoves said: " I never have less than twelve feet height of pipe above the stove. If I can not get it in the room, I put the pipe inside the chimney, and I never fail in getting a good draught."

The Venetians generally use bell-muzzle flues, but they spread more rapidly than Mr. Oldham's proportions.

FIG. 37.—A RURAL RESIDENCE.

DESIGN No. 12.

A RURAL RESIDENCE.

BY CARL PFEIFFER, ARCHITECT, NO. 4 BROAD STREET, NEW YORK.

THIS design is given as one well adapted for a village or rural residence, where economy of space and expense is desired to be combined with an agreeable exterior and appearance of interior spaciousness.

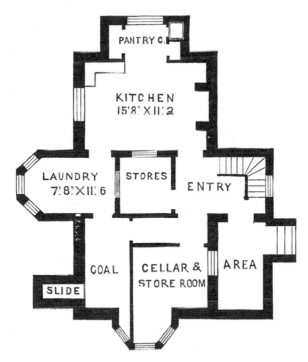

FIG. 38.—BASEMENT PLAN.

This house was built at Hamilton Park, New Brighton, Staten Island, about four years ago, at a cost of six thousand dollars and is one of a group of twelve (all different in design).

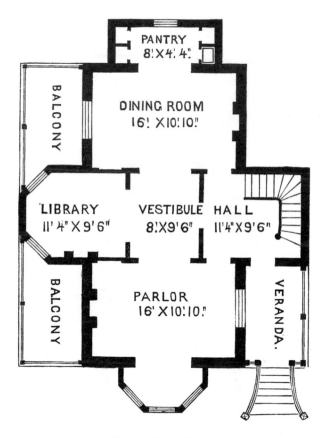

FIG. 39.—FIRST FLOOR.

It is built of brick, with brown stone trimmings and Mansard roof, with slate covering—has a basement, two stories, and an attic; and the attic affords good comfortable rooms, ten feet high, with an air space between the ceilings and roof. The side walls being partly formed by the Mansard roof, are back plastered between the rafters, and the slate is laid upon tarred paper. All these precautions were taken to prevent dampness, heat, and cold from penetrating too readily.

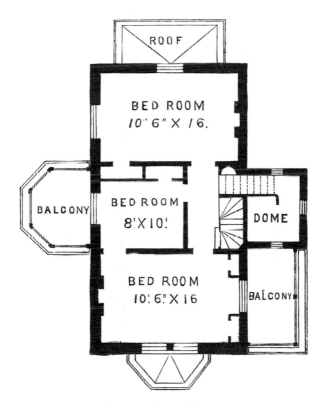

FIG. 40.—SECOND FLOOR.

The basement walls are sixteen inches thick; those above are twelve inches, except the walls of the projections that form the hall and library, which are only eight inches.

The basement contains the kitchen, laundry, and store-rooms. The first story is so arranged that the several rooms communicate by large, double folding doors, and may be opened into one spacious interior, and still are accessible separately.

The projecting part of the library or bay extends up only one story, and forms a balcony in the second story. Though the

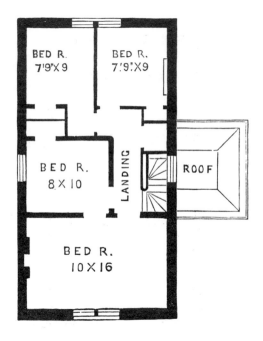

FIG. 41.—ATTIC.

dimensions of the hall are small, a cramped appearance is avoided by the Mansard roof over it forming a dome, giving a ceiling of eighteen feet high to the hall, with colored glass in the skylight and dormer windows.

At the rear of the dining-room a bay is built out, one story high, to afford the closets of a butler's pantry and a dumb-waiter. All may be shut out by large double folding doors opening into the pantry from the dining-room, or the folding doors may be opened, and are so arranged that they will shut against the closets, and give the appearance of a bay window to the pantry corresponding to the bay windows of the parlor when the folding doors between the parlor, vestibule, and dining-room are opened, thus securing on a small scale that appearance of spaciousness so difficult to obtain at a moderate cost.

The second story has three, and the attic four bedrooms, making seven bedrooms in all, and also a number of closets. Added to these, the parlor, library, dining-room, and butler's pantry, of first story, kitchen, laundry, store and cellar rooms in basement, it may readily be seen how it may meet the wishes of a family.

VENTILATION.

BY A. D. G.

IF we mistake not, this subject has already been touched upon in books and papers, but perhaps it will bear another citing. Much as has been said about it, few persons are sensible of its importance. Many are careful to provide excellent food and clothing for themselves and their families; their houses must be handsome and filled with elegant furniture, but as to the quality of the air they inhale, they give themselves little concern.

Providence has surrounded us with an ocean of pure air fifty miles deep, but we bottle up a portion of it and seclude ourselves within it, rendering it poisonous, and then ask one another if this is not domestic comfort? If we exclude air entirely from the lungs longer than three minutes, death will surely follow, but impure air may be breathed for many years, and the patient continue to live. Bad air is a slow poison. That's the trouble; if it only did its work quicker, and in a more striking and conspicuous way, men might be deterred from recklessly breathing it. Those who habitually inhale it are rendered insensible to the sweetness of a pure atmosphere; their taste becomes as vitiated as the air in which they dwell.

If any one doubts the importance of ventilation, we beg to remind him of a few facts. Science tells us that atmospheric air is composed of oxygen gas and nitrogen gas; the former being a supporter of combustion and of animal life, the latter not such a supporter, nor yet positively destructive of either; its office in the animal economy seeming to be to dilute the oxygen which in its pure state would act too powerfully on the system. In the process of respiration, while the nitrogen is given off from the lungs essentially unchanged, the oxygen unites with the carbon of the blood, forming carbonic acid—the same gas which is produced by burning charcoal in the open air—and this poisonous substance constantly being exhaled into the rooms we occupy, it would seem important to dispose of as soon as possible. To this it might be added that more or less excrementitious matter passes off continually by insensible perspiration through the pores of the skin, which is of the same deleterious character, and urges the same plea for ventilation.

We are told, again, that "every twenty-four hours there flow to the lungs sixty hogsheads of air and thirty hogsheads of blood."* What is the design of this? To purify and vitalize the blood. Now, as the health of the body depends largely upon the purity of the blood, and this last upon the purity of the air, we may estimate the importance of looking well to the quality of what we every moment breathe.

And these conclusions of science are confirmed and illustrated by daily observation and experience. Whence come the pale and sallow faces, languid eyes, headaches, catarrhs, debility, coughs, and consumptions which we continually meet with? Whence, chiefly, except from long confinement in the unwholesome air of unventilated houses? And yet we wonder what can be the matter. Are not our dwellings warm and comfortable, and perhaps genteel? We Americans are less robust than our English cousins, men and women. Travelers from abroad, while acknowledging the delicate hot-house beauty of our young ladies, yet tell us our wives and daughters look sickly and frail beside the ruddy, round, elastic figures of their own fair ones.

---

* "Uses and Abuses of Air," by Dr. Griscom, p. 29.

English women live more out of doors, and ventilate their houses better than we do.

In the great majority of our school-houses, work-shops, court-houses, hotels, railway-cars, concert-halls, and churches, the air is unfit for breathing. As a general rule, the windows and doors are kept closed, and the oxygen of the air being rapidly consumed by the burning of many lamps and fires, and by the inspiration of numerous occupants, it is impossible for one to remain long in such places without serious injury to his health. Whence the nausea and headache next morning after concerts and lectures? Whence much of the lassitude, listlessness, and irritability of scholars and teachers? Whence the dullness of sermons and the drowsiness of congregations? True to life is the story of the old Scotch minister who, greatly troubled with the inattention of his auditors, preached to them a series of discourses on "The Sin and Shame o' Sleepin' in Kirks," but without any appreciable improvement of their manners; when, at length, ordering the sexton to partially open several windows during service, the result was all that he could desire.

Time was when our dwellings and public buildings were so constructed that ventilation came as a matter of course. The doors and windows rattled with their looseness. In private houses, the broad fire-place sucked up and carried off the foul air as fast as it was generated. Then, too, men and women lived much in the open air, and were not afraid of it. Now, we make our doors and windows air-tight; our rooms over-heated by air-tight stoves and furnaces; fire-places are seldom seen, or are made for ornament, and closed up with fire-boards; and our food is cooked in air-tight kitchen stoves. These modern improvements cost us dearly, and must continue to do so until we conform more to the laws of health.

In suggesting a few hints as to the best *methods* of ventilation, the writer will speak only of those which may be applied in winter; for in summer, this matter will mostly take care of itself.

To provide fresh air for a dwelling-house, some would say, knock out a panel from every door, and a pane of glass from every window. Others, less heroic, would propose that every door be set ajar often during the day, and that rolling blinds be inserted in every fire-board, to be opened and closed at pleasure. It is an excellent arrangement, also, to insert a register, or a valve like Dr. Arnott's patent, in the chimney-breast near the ceiling, which can be controlled by a simple pulley and cord.

But it is important to bring in a constant supply of fresh air, as well as to expel that which is vitiated by use, and to introduce it in such a way as not to let in also the influenza. When grates are used, it is customary sometimes to introduce a current of out-door air into a hollow space in the chimney, behind the fire, where it becomes warm before entering the room. But for the majority of country houses, grates are the exception, and close stoves the general rule; how, then, can we ventilate rooms warmed by stoves? One simple method is this: Surround a common iron stove with a neat Russia iron case, leaving a space of six inches between the two, and cover the whole at the top with an ornamental grating. Connect this apparatus with the air out of doors by a tin conductor four inches in diameter, leading from a cellar window along under the parlor floor, and then up through the floor into the open space before described. A damper should be inserted in this pipe, to regulate the amount of air brought in. By some arrangement like this, we can introduce a constant supply of pure air, which, when warmed in the air-chamber around the stove, will flow out in a genial current through the perforated top. It is to be supposed, however, that a register or valve is also provided in the chimney flue for carrying off impure air as fast as fresh is brought in.

The grate, or the close stove arranged in the above manner, will answer well when only one or two rooms are to be heated ; but when a whole house or large public building is to be warmed and ventilated, the hot-air furnace will do the work better. (We speak not now of warming by steam or hot water ; for these methods are too expensive for general adoption, and where used do not seem to give entire satisfaction.) The hot-air furnace, properly constructed, with gas-tight joints, and a large copper pan in the air-chamber for evaporating water, provides a constant supply of fresh, summer-like air, and sends the wholesome current, hour after hour, through all the building.

It is, however, an essential requisite of this method of warming a house, that provision be made for a current of air to flow out of every room, as well as one to flow in. Indeed, it is difficult to warm a house in this way, unless some such provision is made. Can you blow wind into a bottle without first displacing an equal portion of the air within it ?* Properly to ventilate a house warmed by a furnace, every room should be provided with a ventilator leading into the chimney flue or into a venti-duct carried up by its side. For, if not so provided, not only will it be hard to force fresh air into the rooms, but that which is forced in will be drawn down again through the registers into the furnace-chamber, whence it will be returned again and again to the apartments for repeated respiration. This is continually occurring in multitudes of houses and public buildings.

---

* Soon after the erection of the splendid edifice for the Smithsonian Institute, it was found impossible to warm one of the large halls of the building so as to make it comfortable. The windows and doors were made air-tight, and the large furnace in the basement was driven up to red heat. Still the air in the lecture-room remained dull and cold—the thermometer indicating only from 45° to 50°. After some time, a man of common sense hearing of the difficulty, called for an auger and hand-saw, with which he soon cut a hole in one corner of the floor, about eighteen inches square. Immediately there was a change in the air—a healthful circulation commenced, and in half an hour the mercury ran up to 75°!

The opening referred to, for the escape of impure air, should be on the side of the room opposite to the register, and should be as near the floor as practicable. If it is made near the ceiling, the freshly-heated air rising at once to the top of the room will pass off through the ventilator and be lost, leaving the cold and impure air near the floor unwarmed and undisturbed ; whereas if the opening were made near the base of the chimney, then the newly warmed air, after first rising to the ceiling, would descend and drive the cold air along the flue up the chimney or ventiduct, and so facilitate both the warming and the ventilating of the apartment. The escape of the vitiated air up the chimney flue would be helped by kindling a small fire on the hearth or in the grate. Indeed, this arrangement— the furnace and a fire on the hearth—constitutes, to our mind, the best known method of warming and ventilating a dwelling-house : the furnace affording a comfortable warmth to the halls and rooms of the entire building, while the ruddy light in the fire-place gives a cheerful, homelike expression to the apartments occupied, which can be gained in no other way; and both together furnishing ample ventilation.

Let it be added, finally, that while specifying these several plans for ventilating buildings, we have desired to suggest correct principles rather than to advocate particular methods.

FIG. 42.—A SUBURBAN HOUSE.

DESIGN No. 13.

A SUBURBAN HOUSE.

THIS house was designed to be erected in the vicinity of a town of considerable importance, having grounds about it of three acres in extent, which are intended to be kept in prime order.

The rooms are arranged compactly, and connect one with another, and the amount of hall room reduced to the least

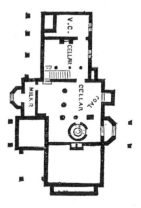

FIG. 43.—CELLAR PLAN.

convenient space. Examples of this style of arrangement are objected to by those accustomed to live in large cities and in the habit of receiving many calls, as the servants, in attending the front door, must pass to and fro through either dining-room or living-room. However objectionable this theory might be in a town house, it amounts to nothing in practice, especially when applied to country residences. The comparative number of visitors is smaller, and only a possible chance exists of both rooms being occupied at the same time in such a manner that the servant's presence would be offensive.

The dining-room is one in which a servant may be found many times during the day, and there can be no more impro-

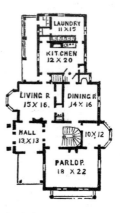

FIG. 44.—FIRST FLOOR.

priety in passing through the dining-room to wait on the front door than in attending to the ordinary duties of the table.

By changing the style of tower, this house could be well adapted for erection on a lot of, say, seventy-five feet front by about two hundred feet in depth.

The plan would be just the one for this purpose, and if hall communication with kitchen be insisted on, this could be obtained by increasing the space between living-room and dining-room, and throwing the living-room farther out from the main building. The tower might then be omitted, and one gable cover both living-room and hall. This would reduce the cost of erection and give an equal amount of available room.

Those who study these plans over for hints for their own use, must not consider the good and defective points of a plan to be inseparable. All these plans admit of infinite changes, and no

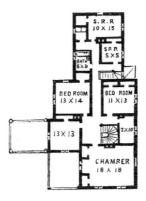

FIG. 45.—SECOND FLOOR.

one person is suited in all respects with a plan adopted by another, however admirable it may be for his purpose, or well adapted to his site and commanding views.

This house is intended to be built of wood, balloon frame, slate roof laid in colored bands, and to be painted a neutral cream color, with two shades of warm brown trimmings; outside of window sashes and outside blinds to be painted a dark bottle green. This will give a rich and imposing effect.

In matter of heating the entire house, the most economical plan would be to procure one of the best furnaces. The largest sizes cost but little more than the small ones, and we should buy at least a size larger than the maker would consider sufficient; the philosophy of this would be, that, in extreme cold weather, we should not be obliged to fire up to full capacity and burn up and vitiate the air with red-hot plates; and, besides, the large furnaces, with large fire boxes, enable a liberal mass of coal to be burned at a very slow rate of combustion, and this will be found to be a matter of economy in fuel. Better to get the heat from a large mass burning slowly than from a small quantity burning rapidly. The atmosphere is better, and the ability to keep the fire over-night and warm the house rapidly in the morning is under thorough control.

Furnaces of small capacity and badly managed produce a dead, dry atmosphere, and are very unsatisfactory; but of liberal size, well provided with evaporating pans, and managed with good judgment, they answer an excellent purpose. Open grates, or registers connecting with ventilating shaft in chimney, should be placed in all rooms in which there is a register from the furnace. A constant movement of the air is very necessary for both heat and health; and it is a question worthy of more consideration whether it is the best practice to build houses so thoroughly air-tight, provide them with double windows, etc., and thus economize fuel and breathe a dull and lifeless atmosphere. Better, we think, on the score of health— for without this nothing will compensate—to lower the ceilings, let doors and windows fit loosely, put an extra scuttle of coal in the furnace, keep a blazing fire on the hearth, and breathe a healthy, living air. Building lower ceilings will economize fuel even more than to build air-tight rooms.

THE FIRE ON THE HEARTH.

AT the inclement season of the year we may well turn our attention from without to within doors, and see by what means we may contrive to make the country home more attractive not only to its inmates, but to the stranger within its walls. And here at the outset, let it be well understood that our suggestions are intended for those who not only live in the country, but whose tastes and predilections are decidedly for rural life. We are writing not only for those who are obliged from circumstances to live in an humble manner, but for those who, with ample means, prefer real solid home comfort to pretense and empty show.

As we can often form an opinion of the character of a man from the expression of his countenance, so, not unfrequently, we are able to judge, from the exterior of a country dwelling, what may be the character of its internal arrangement, and what may be the peculiar tastes of its occupants.

Some homes are so cold and forbidding in their external aspect, that it would seem as if no amount of cheerfulness could ever light up their hearth-stones; while others habitually wear such a smiling and benignant expression, that we long to cross their thresholds and make ourselves familiar with every nook and corner they contain; and is not this the case with old country houses? Is not this their peculiar characteristic? We rarely see one that it does not awaken ideas of true home comfort, which a more modern structure fails to impart; and we think this feeling is common to all persons of cultivation, more especially if they possess strong rural tastes. No matter what may be the peculiar architectural arrangement of the house, if time has mellowed it, this home feeling is almost sure to spring up at first sight. It may be the gambrel roof, with or without its quaint balustrade; it may be the old New England mansion, with its two stories in front, and its roof sloping almost to the ground behind and overshadowed by some venerable elm; or it may be the humble red farm-house, with its moss-covered roof. If these old dwellings possess so winning an exterior, in most cases we are not disappointed on entering them. We shall find that everything within comports with that air of quiet ease and comfort which is inherent, and to which no one thing contributes more than the open chimney-place with its blazing wood-fire. The sight of this makes us perfectly at our ease—we want no more cordial welcome; and herein lies the essence of our present paper—the importance of the fire on the hearth, as a means of imparting health, cheerfulness, and sociability to the inmates of the dwelling.

Let there be one room at least in every home where the family, particularly if there be children, can gather around the chimney-place, and watch, as they sit musing or talking, the flitting flame of either the hickory log, or, for lack of that, the bituminous coal ; and by all means let that fire-place be generous in its size—not, perhaps, so capacious as to allow all to sit within its very jaws, and to look up at the bright stars of heaven shining down from above—such a one we remember, years ago, in a rude cottage in the wilds of Maine, where we passed a night—but still ample enough for a good-sized log to be rolled behind and committed to its bed of ashes.

It is not often that we now see those rousing wood-fires of a former generation. They are no longer an actual necessity. Modern science has introduced many other methods for warding off the searching blasts of winter. The screens that were set up at our backs, as an additional means of attaining warmth and comfort, have now been folded up and laid aside. The in-

numerable logs of wood, usually sawed in the hottest days
of July, by men who were part and parcel of the saw, and who
never tired, however long and hot might be the day, are rarely
wanted now. The large stout leathern apron, with its convenient handles, by which the wood was carried to the fire-
place, is no longer called for.

Our thoughts wander back to youthful days, and we call to
mind a bar-room wood-fire of a country inn in New Hampshire
—a fire which never slumbered night or day through the cold
season, and which was always ready, with its more than genial
warmth, to welcome the shivering stage passenger.

No one of the rising generation, we venture to say, ever saw
such a fire upon the hearth—its huge logs piled one above the
other, and sending up such volumes of flame that no near
approach was possible. That fire has gone out now, and a cold,
black funereal stove has usurped its place. So, too, have gone
out the liberal wood-fires of our fathers' kitchens, before which
were roasted such ample sirloins, and over whose living coals
such savory steaks were prepared.

But if these open fires are no longer a necessity as a means of
affording warmth, are they not necessary as promoters of ventilation, cheerfulness, and gladness in the household? We may
easily decide this by comparing the atmosphere and cheerfulness of a room lighted up by a bright blazing fire, and one
heated only by a furnace or by a closed stove, with every means
of obtaining fresh air carefully cut off. No matter how high
may be the temperature of such a room, if we enter it upon a
cold day, and see no open fire, an involuntary shudder comes
over us—more especially if no rays of sunlight enter to dispel
the gloom.

How pleasant to those who dwell in cities, and who never
know the brightness of a fire on their own hearths, is the recol-
lection of the cosy wood-fire over which they sat in those frosty

evenings of early autumn, following the bright, clear sunny days, in the distant farm-house among the mountains or by the sea-shore ! The thoughts and aspirations of those happy hours will be far more lasting than the embers by the light of which they were kindled.

Let every man, then, who builds or occupies a house, particularly if it be in the country, see that he has at least one open chimney-place or grate for either wood or coal. If he has any desire that his children should ever have happy associations with home, and that in after-years their thoughts should revert with pleasure to the scenes of their youth, let the family fireside be something more than a name. If it be in any way practicable, let there be an open fire-place in every room in the house as a means of ventilation, especially in case of sickness; and in the chamber, what can be more genial or more conducive to that quiet repose which we seek, than watching the fire-light flashing upon the ceiling? and in the tedious hours of illness, what a friend and companion is this same fire-light!

Does not delightful Irving tell us that it was by the light of the open fire that the bold dragoon saw, as he lay snug in bed, the movements of the portrait; and although we may not desire to see anything so terrifying, it is at such times that portrait and picture exert a new influence upon our imagination, however familiar they may be to us. Yes, we should willingly part with many a luxury before we relinquish what we consider a necessity as well as perhaps a luxury.

In the construction of the fire-place in the country house, good, even, well-burnt bricks answer every purpose, not only for the back and jambs, but also for the hearth. Soap-stone as well as freestone are now, however, widely used, and in point of elegance are, perhaps, to be preferred. Tiles of various patterns and colors make very pleasing hearths, which we in every way prefer to marble. If the old Dutch tiles can be procured, let them by all means adorn the fire-place. Your children will form strong associations with their quaint illustrations of Scripture. If they already exist in the old house which you have purchased, consider them as sacred.

In the majority of country dwellings, particularly if they have any claim to antiquity, we should advise the use of wood in the construction of the mantle-piece. It seems far the most appropriate article for the purpose — certainly much more so than marble. The wood may be chestnut, oak, walnut, butternut, or even pine, and it should be simply rubbed down and polished, but never varnished. The mantle-shelf should be deep and capacious, so that the articles placed upon it may not easily be thrown off. It is often, as we well know, a temporary resting-place for almost everything which goes astray. We should not forget to mention those necessary accompaniments to the open fire-place, and which are so intimately associated with it, the andirons, formerly iron, or of highly polished brass or steel, the more or less elaborately constructed fender, and the ever-useful bellows.

Where, from any cause, an open fire-place in the chimney is not practicable, its place may be supplied by the open grate set out into the room, constructed either of soap-stone or of iron. Those known as the Franklin Grate answer an admirable purpose, or, perhaps, still better, those manufactured in Philadelphia.

The closed stove and the furnace are well in their places. As Americans, we must have them, and we confess that they are often extremely convenient and useful, but they should not monopolize every room. If we value the health which good air, cheerfulness, and abundant ventilation are sure to give us and our children, in one apartment at least let us keep up a bright fire on the hearth.

D. D. SLADE, M.D.

Fig. 46. — A Country House - French Roof.

DESIGN No. 14.

A COUNTRY HOUSE.

IN this design we show a French-roofed house, with irregular plan, prepared for erection, by a gentleman of this city, in the vicinity of Llewellyn Park, at Orange, New Jersey. It has some peculiarities about it which have been introduced to suit his taste. It will be noticed there are two principal entrances, one of which in the plan adopted communicates only with the parlor. We have placed a door between the vestibule and stairway, which we think an improvement. From the main hall one is obliged to pass under the stairway before ascending, and in the house as built, this is the only mode of reaching the stairway. The plan is a good one, convenient, and well adapted to command the fine and extensive views of the locality in which it is situated. This house is intended to be built with grout walls, stuccoed, which, if carefully done with good materials, will be permanent and durable; the foundations and cellar walls will be of the best rubble masonry; cellar windows will have stone sills, and the areas about them inclosed with flag stones set on edge. This will enable a good sod to be grown up to the edge, and not die out as when grown on a stone wall.

The parlor windows, of the French or casement style, opening on the piazza, will run to the floor. The bay windows will be finished on sills twenty inches from the floor, and pannelled underneath; the bay window opening from the parlor to be finished without arch; the ceiling of the parlor to run flush out into the bay, and the cornice and enrichments of the parlor ceiling to be continued into and around the bay window.　This gives an impression of size that is utterly destroyed by the use of the arch.

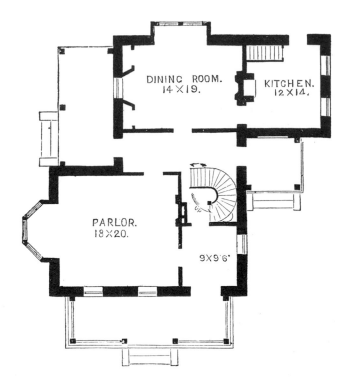

FIG. 47.—FIRST FLOOR.

Bay windows should be boldly treated.　Let the width be eight feet at least, and if ten feet, they would be better.　A half octagon is about the best form; and the exterior appearance is always better if built on foundations instead of hanging.　A hanging or oriel window is usually placed in the second story, and this must necessarily be of smaller dimensions.

In the dining-room, the two closets each side of the end window give an interior appearance of a bay. On the side of the dining-room is a square bay window. This, we think, would be better if projected at least six feet from the face of the wall of the room, and be lighted also from both ends.

In laying the principal floor of a house like this, it would be better, if expense is not too closely considered, to make it double; that is, lay a good ordinary floor, then trim the rooms down to the floor laid; then lay on top another floor of narrow one-and-a-quarter worked and matched pine plank, scribed and fitted snug up to the trimmings. Between the floors lay a good quality of brown paper. This will make tight floors, vermin-proof and air-tight along the base-boards.

In plastering the walls, we would recommend always good three-coat work; and it is better to have quite an interval of time between each coat. This gives an opportunity for settlement, and the final surface will be more free from cracks. Two-coat work is sometimes made use of for the sake of economy, and could hardly be detected by an ordinary observer; but in time the lath will be indicated by parallel lines; and wherever the hard-finish is broken, the friable nature of the first coat yields rapidly and easily to the touch. The first coat, in order to work readily and adhere to the lath, is made with a good deal of lime, and does not become thoroughly hard; the second coat is made with less lime, the least possible amount necessary, and acquires a firm, hard body. On this is placed the hard-finish, and makes a first-rate wall.

Ceilings are—for the cellar, seven feet; first floor, ten and a half feet; second floor, nine and a half feet. These are ample for all purposes of health or ventilation. In fact, these objections against lower ceilings could not be sustained. When ceil-

ings are low, there is a less number of steps to climb, the ability
to heat the house is far easier, and the air of the rooms can be
changed quicker.   Rooms with high ceilings have a finer appearance and accord better with the modern style; there is a

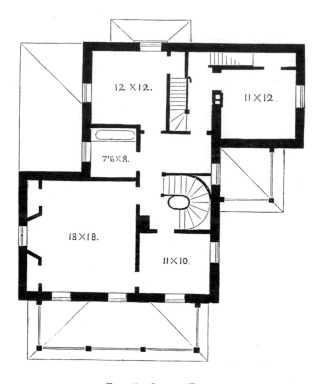

FIG. 48.—SECOND FLOOR.

better opportunity for display of enriched ceilings; and chandeliers, pictures, curtains, etc., show to far better advantage.

As a non-conductor of heat under a slate roof, cork shavings
have been made much use of lately, and with good success.

They are placed in thin layers between the rafters, and can be had at a very moderate price. In finishing the rooms under a French roof, there is an opportunity for ample air-spaces both on the sides and overhead, so that these rooms need not be uncomfortable in warm weather. Slate absorbs heat very rapidly when the sun is shining, and cools quickly after sunset.

Grounds about a house of this character should be very neatly kept. The lawn should be mown frequently, at least once a week during the growing season. A good machine is best for this purpose. It is a good plan to let the clippings remain on the lawn; they disappear in a few hours, and thus the fertility is retained. Frequent rolling is also necessary to keep a fine surface and a thick growth. A well-kept lawn is the finest attraction about a country place, and one that pays well for all the attention bestowed. It need not be large, but should be certainly within such dimensions that shall insure the best care.

Many deem it necessary to spend vast sums in reducing the ground intended for a lawn to a dead level. The natural undulating surface is far more beautiful, and has a productiveness that graded ground will not acquire for many years. The natural soil, once disturbed, is not easily replaced of the same depth, nor will it produce a turf of the same even texture and color. This can readily be seen in seasons of drouth on any lawn made on a graded subsoil. Unless the surrounding grounds are very rough, we should hesitate long before going into extensive removals of earth. It is a very expensive process; and when done, there is nothing to show for it, except to those who knew the ground before the work was commenced.

The general impression is, on moving into the suburbs, that extensive tracts of land are desirable; and when one has been cooped up for years between city walls, he likes to go to the other extreme and have room in abundance. But there are certain habits of order and neatness which business men acquire, which tempt them into all sorts of expenses in keeping their grounds in polished order; and they find out in time that this is by no means an economical proceeding when carried out on a large scale. Well-kept grounds are certainly desirable, and particularly near the house; but they should not be too large

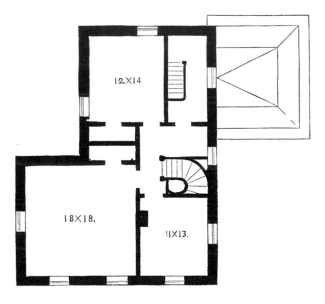

FIG. 49.—ATTIC.

for one's purse. Enjoyment does not increase with the number of laborers employed, or with the number of acres owned; and it is better, under all circumstances, to do well whatever is worth doing at all. We should therefore think from two to four acres enough to occupy all of one's leisure time, and give him an opportunity to spend all the money he wishes to. The question of profit, except in the rise of real estate, can not be entertained. Farming or market gardening are just like any other class of business. He who undertakes either must give his whole attention to it ; cultivating the soil through the agency of the ordinary farm laborer and doing business in town is not a good plan for money getting.

The taste for a suburban residence in the vicinity of a city like New York increases daily. Steam railway accommodation, magnificent cars, and the utmost regularity in time afford facilities for living ten to fifteen miles from business, and going to and fro daily in the same or less time and with far greater comfort than the upper parts of New York or Brooklyn can be reached, and the entire change of air, the rapid ride, and the quiet home in the country give health and strength to grapple with the business of the day.

Twenty years ago a commutation train was not known ; now, from ten to twenty a day leave by every railway, some trains carrying upward of six hundred passengers. The rates are low, the speed rapid, and safety and promptness are all that can be desired. The New Jersey suburbs have the advantage of great accessibility. Steam at once from the business part of the city, and ten miles are passed before horse-cars get above Thirty-fifth Street. In addition, the country is as good, productive, healthy, and desirable, views as fine, and advantages every way fully equal to any of the suburbs in New York State.

FIG. 50.—FRENCH-ROOFED BARN.

DESIGN No. 15.

FRENCH-ROOFED BARN.

WHEN one adopts a style of architecture for his house, barns and outbuildings are generally built after the same model. We could hardly recommend using distinct styles, but think extremes are to be avoided. If one has a French roof to his house, it is by no means necessary to put French-roofed caps on his fence-posts, and a French-roofed barn does not necessarily imply French-roofed summer houses or other small outbuildings. The Mansard roof must not be transferred from its legitimate place and applied to all purposes; its real excellences are thus defeated. For street architecture, it is really one of the finest improvements that has been introduced, and for country houses of ample dimensions it is effective and imposing; and for those poor deluded New Yorkers, so ambitious of constructing three-story freestone fronts in the broad and roomy country, it is just the thing to conceal and apologize for their want of wisdom. It has always been a difficult subject for a city man modeling his country house after his city residence in a brick block, to treat successfully the city cornices and flat roofs, and to him the Mansard roof is a real blessing.

For cottages and small buildings, we do not think it so well adapted. It gives a low, or to use a more expressive phrase, a squatty look; but as fashion, which regulates all tastes, is now setting strongly this way, we suppose the full extreme will be run.

The plan of this barn gives accommodation for three horses,

harness-room, carriages, and a box-stall which ought always to be used when a horse is seldom driven. The very small quantity of exercise that a horse gets even in a box-stall is of great advantage to his health, and his feet keep in much finer condition. We quote the following from a little book called

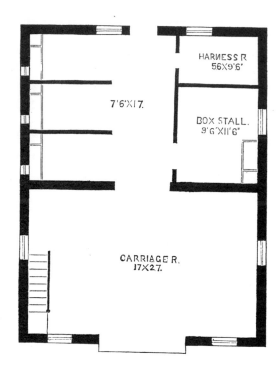

HARNESS R
56X9'6"

7'6"X17.

BOX STALL.
9'6"X11'6"

CARRIAGE R.
17X27.

FIG. 51.—PLAN OF FRENCH-ROOFED BARN.

"Miles on the Horse's Foot," which every horse-owner should have :

"I turn now to the consideration of a subject of fully as much importance to the health and soundness of a horse's foot as good shoeing itself—I mean that inestimable blessing to him, *freedom of motion in the stable.* The advantages of a loose box are so little understood by horse-masters in general, that its usefulness is almost entirely limited in their estimation to sickness and disease; and it is no uncommon sight to behold two or three loose boxes untenanted, because, forsooth, there are no sick horses in the stud.

"I was first led to divide my stable into boxes instead of stalls from motives of compassion for my horse, and a desire to rid myself of the uncomfortable feeling it always produces in me, to see so docile and generous an animal subject to even greater restraint than a wild beast in a menagerie; for the lion or tiger is permitted freely to traverse his small den, while the poor horse is chained by the head to a fixed point in his still smaller den, a prisoner twice imprisoned, and denied even the poor relief afforded by a change of position. I little thought, while thus solely bent upon ministering to my horse's comfort, how essentially I was furthering my own interest, until an accident brought me acquainted with Mr. James Turner's invaluable treatise on the foot of the horse, where I first learned, what subsequent experience has fully confirmed to me, the wonderful extent to which the usefulness of the horse is *secured and prolonged* by the freedom of motion obtained in a loose box. We have already seen how materially his usefulness is impaired by the smallest injury to the navicular joint; and we have also seen the beautiful provision nature has made for its protection from injury in the elastic cushion interposed between it and the horny frog. It shall now be my endeavor to show in what manner a loose box tends to keep this cushion in a healthy state of elasticity.

" Nature forms nothing in vain; all her works are designed for specific purposes; each organ has its separate function assigned to it; and the only condition upon which she will consent to keep it in efficient repair, is the regular and periodical performance of that function. For instance, suppose an accident deprive a man of the use of his arm for a few months; the muscles at the end of that period will be found visibly shrunk, and the whole arm considerably smaller than its companion, constituting, in horsemen's language, 'a very bad match.' Here the non-employment of the muscles has accelerated the process of absorption, while that of restoration has been nearly suspended. The muscles of the other arm, on the contrary, being regularly employed, have earned and received their due measure of restoration, and retain their original dimensions; and so it is with the elastic cushion in the horse's foot; if we deprive the horse of the power of alternately expanding and contracting his foot, as nature intended he should do, this cushion will shrink and lose its elasticity; but if we supply him with the means of doing so, he will avail himself of them, and its elasticity will be retained to a good old age.

"The almost perpetual movement of a horse in a state of nature, while grazing, greatly tends to preserve the different elastic parts of his foot in a sound and healthy condition, by the regular compression and expansion which they undergo, according as his weight is thrown upon or removed from them; but if we chain him to a post for twenty-two out of every twenty-four hours, we can scarcely wonder that so unnatural a proceeding should derange an organ that requires motion to preserve it in health. Take, in illustration of the mischievous tendency of this practice, the horses of a cavalry regiment: they have everything in favor of sound feet except the *stall* and the *rack chain;* they are entirely exempt from the hard work which is generally referred to as the cause of grogginess; they have no oft-repeated and long journeys to perform at a fast pace on the hard road; their exercise, shoeing, grooming, and feeding are all administered with clock-work regularity; the litter is carefully removed from under their feet during the day; the veterinary surgeon is always at hand to attend to the first symptom of lameness; and still there are more horses cast as unserviceable every year from disabilities commencing in the foot than from all other causes combined. The *rest*, and not the *work*, has wrought the ill. Now let us see how loose boxes are to prevent these evils. When a horse is free to move, he very rarely remains long in the same place or the same position; he is perpetually turning himself about, either to catch a distant sound or observe an approaching footstep; everything attracts him; everything interests him; and, what is of far greater moment, everything causes him to *move;* whereby each foot is benefited to the extent of some four or five expansions and contractions; and the sound of the corn-bin at feeding-time will produce at least fifty such. It is far otherwise with the poor beast chained up in a stall; he is attracted by the same sounds; hears the same step approach; and feels the same interest: he pricks his ears, bends his head, and strains his neck; but, alas! he does not move; his feet are not expanded; turning about he knows to be impossible, and therefore he does not attempt it; even the sound of the corn-bin, though it excite him to jump and play, will scarcely cause him to expand his feet; the excitement inclines him to rush forward, while the wall forbids him to comply; and he is forced to collect himself, so as to throw his weight upon his hind quarters, almost to the entire exclusion of the fore feet. Horses accustomed to a loose box generally acquire a slow, deliberate movement in it, allowing their weight to dwell evenly and fully upon each fore foot; while those kept in a stall for the most part move in it with a quick, sudden, catching motion, scarcely ever intrusting their whole weight to either foot for more than an instant."

FIG. 52.—HOUSE WITH ITALIAN ROOF.

DESIGN No. 16.

HOUSE WITH ITALIAN ROOF.

THIS house is designed for erection on the banks of the Passaic River, one of the most beautiful rivers in this country. It probably can not be surpassed in its attractions by any one of similar length, and yet is but little known to the outside world. The source and feeders of this miniature Hudson are mountain springs, and its course to the sea is rapid and over rock and gravel bottoms, winding by fertile farms, magnificent country seats, and flourishing cities.   Although but about forty miles in length, and navigable for two-hundred-ton schooners but one third this distance, there is living on its banks, and within a mile of the river, a population of 200,000.

The drive along cither bank from Newark to Passaic, is one of the most delightful we know of—and this part of the river has a destiny that few are aware of; any portion of it can be reached in from forty to sixty minutes from Broadway, hourly, by several lines of railway.

It has long been the resort of wealthy New Yorkers and their princely palace homes line the banks for many miles. These large estates are now yielding to the overflow demand of New York city, and are being divided into small tracts and suburban lots, which are rapidly taken up and improved. Magnificent avenues are opened, public houses built on a grand scale, and on all sides country homes are being erected for New York business men, from the modest cottage to the roomy mansion;

and they can live on the banks of this beautiful river, and on its wood-crowned heights, and go hourly to their business in town, or drive the eight to ten miles to the ferries whenever it suits their convenience.

The history of the large fortunes of the old families of the city of New York has been in the rise of real estate; city lots have proved to be gold mines which, in spite of all contrary predictions, have annually accumulated values which have in the course of years exceeded investments of all other descriptions. What has already transpired within the city limits is now taking place throughout all its suburbs, for the growth of these have been beyond all precedent, not only from their natural increase, but from the overflowing thousands unwilling to accept crowded accommodations in the city. It may surprise some to hear that the population of the suburbs of New York, within twenty-five miles, exceeds that of the city itself, and that round the center of this great commercial metropolis has already gathered a population rising 2,000,000, and that an annual substantial increase, reliable and unvarying, of 100,000 persons is constantly being added to the numbers already here. More than 8,000 persons per month are making their permanent homes within the twenty-five-mile circle around and in the city of New York; and this is but the average annual percentage of increase which with almost unvarying regularity has been going on for fifty years. For the future, however, this growth will be mainly in the suburbs, which are ramified in all directions by railroads; and he who has courage to invest in real estate, improve it, and hold on to it, will in time realize his grandest conception of a fortune. The points are all good and some least known are better than others; those most accessible in the shortest time and with the most liberal accommodation will realize the largest results. There are golden opportunities now lying unembraced whose promises exceed the richest realizations of the past.

The main part of this house is forty by thirty-five feet, with hall running through the center, and principal rooms laid off on

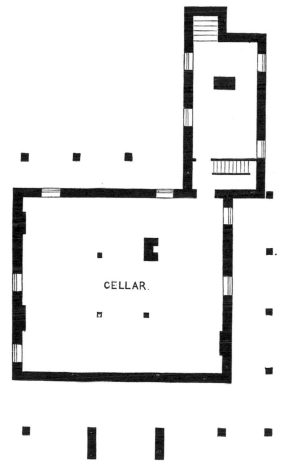

CELLAR.

FIG. 53.—CELLAR PLAN.

each side. There is nothing particularly new in the arrangement, but it affords a great amount of accommodation, and in a form, all things considered, the most economical. The finest country houses we know of are similarly arranged on the square or long square plan, with kitchen and servants' apartments in a wing by themselves, where cross ventilation is complete, and where odors and noise produce no annoyance. On the second floor, the bath-room is placed at the remote end of the rear building, over the laundry. This confines all the plumbing apparatus in the whole house to a very small space. Range, boiler, laundry tubs, etc., being immediately under the bath-room, and waste and supply pipes passing through a recess in the kitchen chimney, protects all against frost. This plan may be objected to on account of distance of bath-room from sleeping apartments. It has its good points, however, and not the least is that the parlor ceilings, pictures, and carpets are free from danger of flooding by bursting of pipes on a frosty night or from other causes, which increase with the length of pipe and distance from boiler.

This house is to be built with the balloon frame, it being the strongest, and forty per cent. cheaper than the old-fashioned mortice and tenon frame; and among intelligent builders is as rapidly taking the lead here, as it has done years ago throughout the West and on the Pacific coast. Old-fogy builders who are averse to learn anything new, are yielding to a belief in its merits; the rapidity with which it can be put up, the labor and expense saved, and strength and solidity it maintains, are advantages which can not be undervalued. Let one of our old-fashioned Eastern mechanics, who has traveled in one rut all his life, go to Chicago, or to any wide-awake Western town, and talk about heavy timber, mortices and tenons, square rule, etc., and he will find himself quite as entertaining and as much a subject of wonder as Rip Van Winkle was when he came down from the mountains after his twenty years' sleep. If he expects to get work, he must shave, dress himself in modern style, clear

away the cobwebs, and adopt the progressive ideas and enterprise of the West. There, where they build the largest and most

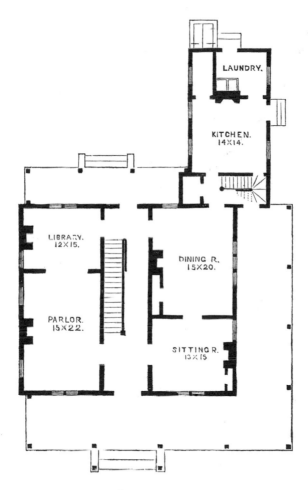

FIG. 54.—FIRST FLOOR.

magnificent frame houses on the continent, the balloon frame is
the only frame known. It has been tested in every form and

style through long series of years, and universally adopted by all who build.

The balloon frame is without mortice, tenon, or brace. It is put up stick by stick. A mechanic with a good smart boy or a common laborer can build the largest frame, and all extra assistance for the purpose of hurrying the work need only be that of laborers skillful enough to saw wood. In a former volume, " Woodward's Country Homes," the details of constructing these frames are fully illustrated and described.

In these days of high prices, any sound improvement that tends to economize is worthy of consideration, and in connection herewith we will mention one item where not only first expense is saved, but a large amount of labor for all time afterward. The expense of digging and fitting up a well forty feet in depth, in the suburban districts of this city, does not differ now materially from $500. The expense of increasing the size of a cistern to hold from six to eight thousand gallons is a very small item. If the roof be tin or slate, the rain water which comes from it will be of crystal purity. If a shingle roof, the water will be slightly discolored, generally a yellowish tinge ; and the common impression is that the natural color of rain water is yellow, and its natural taste that imparted to it by the shingles. If rain water from a shingle roof is used for drinking purposes, it should be filtered ; if from a slate or metal roof, filtering is not necessary ; the water rivals in transparent brilliancy and purity that of the finest well or spring, and in healthy qualities has no superior ; in winter the temperature is right, and in summer it requires the addition of ice. For all culinary purposes, and especially in making tea and coffee, it is by far the best. For the preservation of the fine coat on race-horses, rain water is sometimes carried long distances ; and those cities of Europe using rain water only, have never been visited by the cholera. But, says one, rain water is flat to the taste ; yet no visitor of ours has ever discovered it until told he was drinking rain water. New Yorkers pride themselves on the Croton, and turn

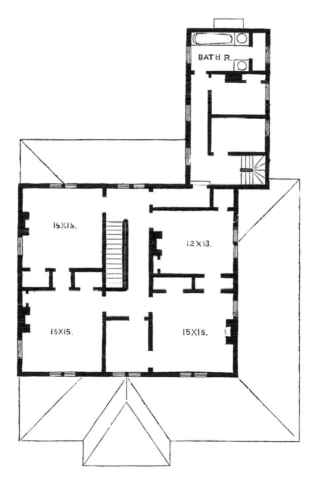

FIG. 55.—SECOND FLOOR.

up their noses in horror at rain water—and so they might if they had it from their own dusty, coal-begrimed roofs. With remarkable freshness they live in filthy streets, breathe all sorts of foul odors, and innocently ask if the country is healthy.

Any argument that can be brought against the full use of rain water for all purposes must be based on prejudice. If it were worth while, we could further sustain our point by authorities innumerable, but we have said enough to attract attention from those inclined to further investigation. Now as to the convenience. We have found in several years' experience that a moderate-sized family with garden, two horses, and two cows are amply supplied, and through long seasons of drought, by a cistern holding 6,000 gallons. A pump in the house, one in the barn, and one in the garden, may all draw from the same source. The water is conveniently at hand, and no running out in bad weather to hoist it forty or fifty feet and to carry it back slopping to the house; the pump responds easily and quickly, and the water coming from a moderate depth, lightens the labors and saves time and steps to both household and outside help. How many we know that might almost save the yearly labor of one person, especially where large numbers of cattle and horses are kept, by a proper arrangement of facilities for procuring water easily! How many families in the country would be accommodated to a degree now unknown if water could be had by the least possible effort! With all the bounteous provisions of nature, few know or care to know how easy it is to lighten their labors not only in this respect, but in numberless other instances. All of one's life will be spent in endless drudgery that the opening of a single door would reduce one half. Steps innumerable could be saved every year by adopting a well-studied plan, and that which is now hard and discouraging might be made easy and agreeable with no additional expense. In all cases, a plan should be first prepared, no matter how small the building may be; draw it yourself, no matter how roughly, rather than not have one; then study it, change it, reconstruct it, until every convenience has its proper place and its proper combination; have a place for everything required, and prepare, at the proper season, all things needed when inclement weather comes on. Water, wood, coal, etc., should be at hand under cover, and in condition for immediate use. A good house-drain should be provided, of ample dimensions, and sufficient descent to prevent clogging. Vitrified pipe, six inches in diameter, leading off one hundred feet to a cesspool in the garden, where wash, bath, and dish water can accumulate, for use as liquid manure; this drain, properly laid and trapped, will be found a profitable investment, and the back-door approach in consequence can be kept as unexceptionally neat as any other portion of the premises. The drain will carry off everything objectionable, except that which usually goes to the pigs, and will be found indispensable to all who have once had this convenience. Stationary wash-tubs, which may be supplied either by tank or cistern-pump and waste into the drain, will save a good deal of hard labor. If built of good plank, with joints set in white lead, they will last many years, and cost but little if anything more than the ordinary portable tub. These and many other handy contrivances of modern life should all be thoroughly considered by those who wish to make labor light and life easy.

FIG. 56.—FRONT ELEVATION OF A FLAT-ROOFED BARN.

FIG. 57.—SIDE ELEVATION OF A FLAT-ROOFED BARN.

DESIGN No. 17.

A FLAT-ROOF BARN.

THE accompanying design for a stable was made for erection in connection with the house just described, and is as economical as any plan or style of building that can be adopted. Square buildings, of good proportions, with broad projecting roofs, judiciously painted with strong contrasts between the body and trimmings, always look well. The derisive comparison with a cubical box, in which some writers indulge, fails to maintain its point when practically demonstrated. The square, or long square, form of plan has its merits, and will always stand among the best of all forms that can be suggested. It wears well, bears abuse well, is economical, roomy, convenient, imposing. We give herewith a copy of the specifications, which detail all particulars.

SPECIFICATIONS FOR SUPPLY OF MATERIALS AND THE CONSTRUCTION OF A BARN.

EXCAVATION.—Excavate trenches for foundation wall two and one half feet deep, and wide enough to lay a wall twenty inches wide. Remove such earth as is required beneath the stalls, and for gutter, drains, and cesspool. Dig trench for pump pipe to connect with cistern at the house. Do all grading necessary to finish up after the mason work.

MASONRY.—Build a foundation wall three feet high and twenty inches wide, pointed outside, above ground, of good rubble stone, laid in mortar; build two piers to support

girders for floor. Pave with broken stone, two and a
quarter inches cube, and grout and cement thoroughly
the ground floor of horse stalls, giving a slope of four
inches from head of stall to the gutter. Form a gutter
in same manner and with same slope. Lay a vitrified

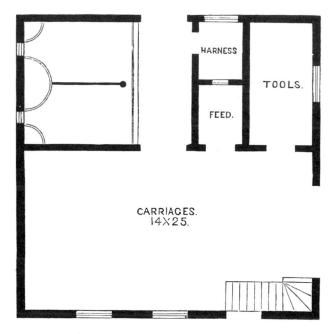

FIG. 58.—FIRST FLOOR.

drain pipe from gutter to cesspool. Build cesspool of
stone laid in mortar, and cement the same two coats,
making it tight, and provide a flag-stone cover. Lay a
suitable drain to carry off rain water. Lath and plaster
two coats, and skim the coachman's room, walls and
ceiling.

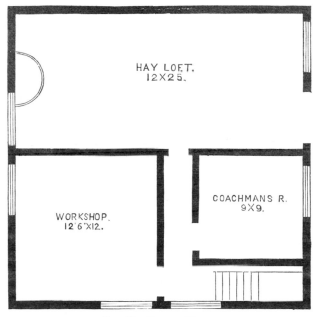

FIG. 59.—SECOND FLOOR.

CARPENTER WORK.

FRAME.—Balloon style.

Sills,   3 by 9.

Floor-beams, 3 by 9, with girder 6 by 8 through the center, supported on piers for first floor.   Lay floor-
beams one foot apart.

Support second floor by girder 6 by 8 inches, and lay
floor-beams 3 by 9, 16 inches apart.

Corner studs, 4 by 6.

Other studs, 3 by 4.

Plates,   3 by 4.

Rafters,   4 by 6.

Side girts,   1 by 6.

All thoroughly nailed.

FLOORING.—Lay first floor, except stalls, with wide one-and-a-quarter-inch matched unworked spruce plank.

Lay second floor with wide matched and worked pine boards.

ROOFING boards to be same as second floor.

SIDING to be narrow lap, laid horizontally, corner boards and base one-and-a-quarter-inch pine.

VENTILATOR.—Frame and build ventilator as shown.

PARTITIONS—Except for coachman's room, to be spruce boards, matched and laid horizontally to studs.   Coachman's room to be trimmed and finished.

STAIRWAY.—Build stairway as shown—seven inches tread, nine and a half inches rise, plain, unworked one-and-a-quarter-inch plank.

CLOSETS.—Build harness, feed, and tool closets as shown, and fit them up as directed by owner.

STALLS.—Build a movable sparred floor for stalls, reaching from head of stall beyond and covering the gutter.   This floor will be built of spars two by four inches, laid lengthwise of stalls, and one fourth of an inch apart, attached to battens, three in number, laid crosswise of stalls, and of such thickness as shall give a level surface when laid on the sloping cemented floor.   The drainage passes through and into the gutter beneath.   See detail drawings.

FIG. 60.

FIG. 61.

FEED-BOX.—Provide and set a corner iron feed-box of largest size in each stall.

HAY-SHOOT.—Ceil up with narrow plank a semicircular shoot for hay, reaching up to two feet above second floor. Provide an opening from each stall for horse to feed from.

WINDOWS.—Hinge the window sash at the head of each stall, and provide each with long iron hook. All others on first floor to be double hung and provided with fastenings.

On second floor to be hinged at bottom and furnished with suitable fastenings.

DOORS.—Outside doors to be built as shown, suitably hung, and provided with good, substantial locks; good four-panneled doors for rooms on second floor, with locks.

TINNING.—Roof to be covered with best quality of tin; gutters to be formed and leaders of suitable size provided and set, sufficient to carry all the water to drain. All tin work to be painted two coats of paint suitable for the purpose.

PUMPS.—Provide a good cast-iron suction pump for barn, and set the same for use where directed. Connect the same by lead pipe, laid below frost, with the cistern at the house. Make and set up a suitable drinking-trough.

Provide, set, and connect for use a good cast-iron suction pump and lead pipe, on top of cesspool, for liquid manure.

PAINTING.—All outside wood-work, and the wood-work of coachman's room to be painted two coats, best white lead and oil, with such tints as directed by owner.

WORKMANSHIP—Throughout to be of the best class.

FINALLY—Completely finish the building for occupancy, to the full intent and meaning of plans and specifications, and satisfactory to the owner or his agent.

FIG. 62.—FRENCH-ROOFED FARM-HOUSE.

DESIGN No. 18.

FRENCH-ROOFED FARM-HOUSE.

IN this design we show a house erected during the past summer at Orange, N. J. It is a one-story, French roof, and is intended for a farm-house. It is situated on the right of the railroad going west; in the rear are the Orange Mountains, and to the right is Llewellyn Park, with its many attractive beauties, designed and developed as one of the most beautiful of all of the suburbs of New York. The influence this Park has had on all the surrounding country could hardly be estimated. The taste, skill, and energy of Mr. Haskell has developed not only a fortune for himself, but he has made fortune after fortune for the original owners of the soil, and for all who had foresight enough to go into the same locality and help improve and build it up. The people of Orange, and of the State of New Jersey, and the owners of the Morris and Essex Railroad, are under obligations to him that they can never repay. He has added a wealth to the State and a business to that community that will continue to flourish long after he has passed away.

It is astonishing how much a man of energy and talent can accomplish when he resolutely sets to work to build up a community; how few and distrustful are his friends, but how rapidly they rally around his banner with the first note of success! and if the first principles are correct, this success will come at last, if pursued with unceasing and untiring perseverance. There are few pioneers in this world, but the followers are numerous, and he who leads must demonstrate by acts his confidence and belief. The first development of any plan of improvement is always the most difficult, and that which must be undertaken almost alone by its projectors. But let the successful point be once reached, then further progress is comparatively easy. What has been accomplished at Llewellyn Park is now being repeated,

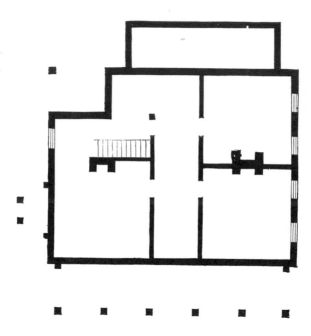

FIG. 63.—CELLAR PLAN.

with some slight alterations of plan, in numerous localities about this city; but the main difficulty seems to be that the great mass who seek these elysian retreats from the whirl of business, are in utter ignorance of their location. Landed proprietors and railway managers have not yet awakened to the value of advertising. There is no surer road to success, no better indication of spirit, than to keep persistently before the public eye the merits of a really sound enterprise.

The plans of this house are arranged so as to provide all necessary conveniences that the best class of farm-houses should have. Wood, coal, water, etc., are under cover and easy of access, and ample parlor and living room suggest a higher grade of life and enjoyment.

There is great difficulty in the successful treatment of a one-story house with this style of roof. It will have a low look in spite of all that can be done. This, however, looks well, and may be considered a good example of the class it represents.

The chimneys are carried up to a good height above the roof, which will give a better draught; and while the subject of chimneys suggests itself, we will make an extract from a valuable little work recently published in Boston, by Messrs. A. Williams & Co., called "The Chemistry of the Farm and the Sea," by James R. Nichols, M.D., editor of the Boston *Journal of Chemistry*. The book is one that all should possess and read, and the articles are sound, valuable, and full of interest. This extract is from the article called "The Chemistry of the Dwelling."

"Simple as is the contrivance of a chimney, it is singular they should be a modern invention. There is no record of any chimney being used in dwellings prior to the twelfth century, and even as late as the time of Queen Elizabeth they were quite uncommon in England. It is stated that Good Queen Bess herself resided in a room unprovided with the luxury of a chimney. They were undoubtedly in use in Venice in the middle of the thirteenth century, and in Padua, but not in Rome; for when, in 1368, Cararo, lord of the first-named city, visited Rome, he found no chimneys in the inn where he lodged, and his host kindled a fire in a hole in the middle of the floor for his comfort, or rather discomfort. The buried cities of Italy afford no evidence that chimneys were used by the ancient Romans, as no contrivance has yet been discovered in either Pompeii or Herculaneum designed to carry away the products of combustion. Before the construction of chimneys, the smoke was allowed to escape through an orifice in the side or top of the room. And in the imperfectly constructed dwellings of those times there

FIG. 64.—FIRST FLOOR.

were plenty of vents for the ingress of air, so that smoke and gases were diluted and rendered comparatively innocuous.

"We may almost presume that smoke was a *luxury* in those early days; the people certainly regarded a smoke-impregnated atmosphere as a healthful one. Old Hollingshed, an Englishman, who wrote several centuries since, thus complains of the innovation of chimneys :

" 'Now we have many chimneys, yet our tenderlings do complain of rheums and catarrh and poses. Once we had nought but a rere-dose (a fire-place), and our heads did never ake, for the smoke of those days was a good hardening for the house, and a far better medicine to keep the good man and his family from the quack or pose, with which then very few were acquainted. There are old men yet dwelling in the village where I remain, who have noted how the multitude of chimneys do increase, whereas in their young days there were not above two or three, if so many, in some uplandish towns of the realm. And peradventure in the manor places of some great lordes, but each one made his fire against a rere-dose, in the hall where he dined and dressed his meat.

" 'But when our houses were built of willow, then we had oaken men ; but now our houses are built of oak, our men are not only become willow, but a great many altogether men of straw, which is a sore alteration.'

" The quaint, humorous old writer would be called a ' croaker' in these days. He was evidently one of those who believed in the rapid deterioration of the race, and was disposed to charge it to the effeminacy of the times, by which many were led to refuse to breathe an atmosphere saturated with smoke and cinders—a philosophy worthy of the fourteenth century. While it was possible to dispense with chimneys, so long as wood alone formed the only combustible material, the introduction of coal at once rendered them indispensable. The large quantity of volatile sulphureted gases which are formed by the heat, and which pass off from soft coals, together with the carbonic acid gas proceeding from all varieties, would render rooms positively uninhabitable were no chimneys in use. The visible smoke proceeding from burning wood, composed as it is mostly of fine cinders and unchanged particles of the wood, is not poisonous, but in a very considerable degree irritating to the mucous membrane of the air-passages of the mouth and nose, and also to the eyes.

" Hence those living in smoky houses have the impression that

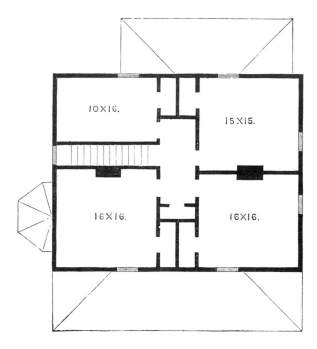

FIG. 65.—SECOND FLOOR.

they are troubled with continued catarrh or colds, the irritability produced by smoke resembling so closely that resulting from this affection. Notwithstanding the statements of Hollingshed, our experience leads us to believe that the lungs are rendered more sensitive to atmospheric changes by the frequent inhalation of smoke; and those compelled to live in a smoky atmosphere are more troubled with 'rheums and catarrh and poses' than those who do not.

"One thing is certain—no annoyance is regarded as more severe than a smoky house; and if the ancient philosophy of the 'hardening' process was correct, few would submit to it for the benefits conferred. How to make a chimney draw well is a question of the first importance with thousands, and one to which the sagacious Franklin early directed his attention. He was regarded in England at one time as the most accomplished 'smoke doctor' living, and his advice was sought upon the subject of draught in chimneys with great frequency.

"A few simple principles are worth remembering respecting the *cause* of draught and methods of increasing it. If a chimney is constructed of any height and dimensions, it is of course filled with air. And if the column of air within it weighs as much as a column of equal height surrounding it without, it will have no draught. Two things operate to change the relation of the columns, and create an ascensional current within the chimney. One is elevation or height; the other, warming the air by fire, by which it becomes rarefied and its weight diminished. The taller the chimney, or the hotter the fire, the more rapid will be the draught. It must be constructed vertically, as much length horizontally, by cooling the air before it gets into the effective part of the flue, will be sure to spoil the draught.

"If a grate or fire-place is troublesome by reason of incompetency to convey away smoke, it may be owing to too great an aperture above the fire, so that a large volume of cold air enters the flue without passing through it, and thus is constantly cooled. A stove connecting with it would work satisfactorily, because the air would be compelled to pass through the fire, and thus keep the chimney current warm and active. A sliding valve, so arranged as to increase or diminish this orifice *above* the fire, is often a complete remedy.

"Chimneys upon the north part of a building do not uniformly work as well as others, because of the refrigerating influences of the locality. A chimney thus situated may be made successful by constructing it double, or making an air chamber around it to preserve warmth. Blocks of buildings are much freer from smoke annoyances, because of the multiplicity of flues, which diffuse a constant warmth through the walls in which they are constructed.

"There must be a sufficient supply of air flowing into the parlor to maintain vigorous combustion, else there will be defective draught. If there is a want of air, the current in the chimney will be reversed, and will flow downward instead of upward. Tightly fitting double windows, with doors listed and weather strips at the bottom—how can rooms thus situated receive a proper supply of air? Not only will the fire upon the hearth go out, but the unseen fires within the bosoms of the occupants of the parlor will lose their glow, and expire. One great source of smoky chimneys in city and country is the contiguity of high buildings or hills by which their tops are commanded. The smoke in such cases is beaten down by the rush of wind over them, like water over a fall. In such instances, one of two things must be done—the flue must be raised higher than the eminence, or resort must be had to somebody's patent cowl or revolving bonnet, a contrivance in such general use in cities that the lines of flues, viewed from an elevated point, look like regiments of grim warriors, with their heads dressed in ugly, fantastic gear, nodding and twirling in the wind. An immense amount of human contrivance has been expended in alterations and modifications of these appendages, as the records of our Patent Office clearly prove. And, after all, the whole matter is comprehended in the simple attachment to the flue of a rotating bonnet, so that in whatever direction the wind blows, its mouth may be averted from it. There are chimneys which set all ingenuity at defiance, and smoke on and smoke ever, although the money expended upon them in attempts to remedy the evil may almost exceed the cost of the building of which they form an ungracious part.

"Dr. Franklin, when in London, was himself thwarted in attempts to cure one of these obstinate flues. After exhausting his practiced philosophy upon it, his friend, the owner of the dwelling, discovered it filled with birds' nests, upon the removal of which the evil was instantly abated.

"Smoke, as we have already stated, is nothing but fuel in a minutely subdivided state, and therefore it should be burned instead of being allowed to make its exit from the fire unconsumed. Numerous devices have been urged upon the public for the accomplishment of this object, but they are all defective in their practical workings. In large manufacturing establishments in England the burning of the smoke is common; and it would indeed be a desideratum if this result could be extended to the fires of private dwellings, as, in addition to the removal of a nuisance, there would be a considerable saving of fuel in the process. The inventive faculty can hardly be employed upon a more worthy or philanthropic object."

FIG. 66.—A GOTHIC FARM-HOUSE.

DESIGN No. 19.

A GOTHIC FARM-HOUSE.

THIS house was erected after plans prepared by us, and is a good example of a solid, substantial farm-house, built and occupied by one of the most prominent and successful farmers of this State, and within a stone's throw of the original dwelling put up by him nearly fifty years before, when he commenced to reclaim from the wilderness what now is one of the most superb and productive farms in the country—a farm that, by good sound management, has been kept up to a high state of fertility, and has made the fortune of the owner.

This house is built of stone, a hard, rock-faced granite, selected and collected during a long series of years. The mason-work is a model, and executed with a degree of care, skill, and fairness such as is rarely met with. One may look in vain among our most costly mansions and not see work that will compare with it. Carpenter work and materials are the best of their class, and the house is one that will do credit to builders and proprietors.

The cellar is constructed only under the main building, the rear addition having foundation walls, a large cellar not being needed, as abundant room of this kind had been provided under the farm buildings. We are, however, of the opinion, after having twice built for our own use, as well as for others, that we should in no further instance neglect to advise the construction of a cellar under the whole house, no matter how small an amount of cellar room would answer. It is difficult to decide what may be one's future wants even in this respect. Certainly it is better to be able at all times to sweep out, clean up, whitewash, etc., under the whole house. A foundation is an inaccessible place, but one of great resort for rats, cats, and all

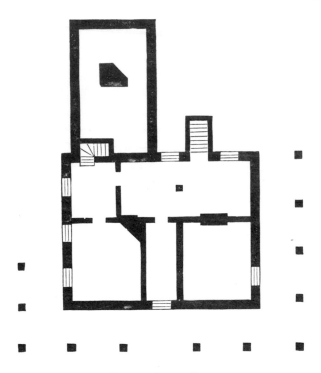

FIG. 67.—CELLAR PLAN.

classes of vermin. It is very desirable at all times to be able to get at the under part of the entire first floor. Bell-wires, furnace-tubes, ash-pits, and other necessary conveniences will sometimes get out of order, and should easily be got at. Ventilation is also an item of importance, and convenient access should be had to all cellar windows. Much has been written to show that cellars are unhealthy ; but if properly constructed, finished, and cared for, we see no good reason why they should be. If the soil is the least retentive of moisture, a good drain should be provided. The cellar floor should be grouted and cemented; this will prevent dampness from rising. Good thorough circulation of air should be maintained by cross-drafts through the windows, and each chimney should be provided with one ventilating flue from the cellar. Care should be taken that no decaying vegetables are allowed to remain, and that a perfect system of neatness at all times be maintained.

The walls of this house being of stone, the first courses above ground were laid in cement, to prevent, as far as possible, the ascent of dampness. Between the stone work and the plastered walls is an air-space, produced by furring out with two-by four studding, to which the lath are nailed ; this air-space prevents outside dampness from striking through into the room, and should always be done in houses built of stone or brick. Hollow brick walls should be furred out, as the binders convey moisture from outside to inside; and though it is contended they do not need it, we have never seen a hollow brick wall that did not dampen the plaster laid on to it. The dead air-space adds much to the warmth and comfort of a house. We have seen many examples of furring out by constructing a brick wall four inches from the face of the stone wall and fastened to it by iron anchors. This plan of furring out is used in large and expensive houses, and adds very much to their fire-proof qualities, as well as to their cost and endurance.

The plans of this house, or the arrangement of rooms, closets, and other conveniences, were marked out by the owner, and he expresses full satisfaction of their entire fitness and comfort. We give in all our plans the sizes and names of the principal rooms, so that it is scarcely necessary to describe them in detail.

One can, by careful examination, thoroughly understand the sizes and position of each apartment, and with ordinary ingenuity adapt a plan for their own wants. Practical hints of this character will be found a valuable aid in making up the

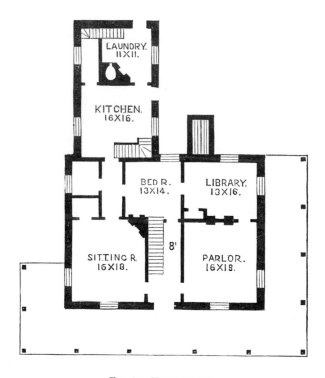

FIG. 68.—FIRST FLOOR.

plan best suited to the exposures and conveniences of a different site.

We intended, in this work, to yield to a popular demand for estimates of cost ; but on further reflection must adhere to the opinions hitherto expressed. Prices are local. The circulation of this book, like our previous publications, will be not only national but world-wide, and a New York estimate is valueless at remote points; indeed, there is a wide difference in prices between points fifty miles west and fifty miles north of this city. A good local mechanic should be able to give an approximate estimate from the plans and perspective view as shown in this book. As a general thing, however, these houses in this vicinity would cost from five to seven dollars per square foot of plan; that is, a two-story cottage, thirty feet square, would have 900 square feet of plan, which at five dollars a foot would be $4,500; and in localities where lumber and labor are cheaper, and a plainer style of finish would answer, three dollars per square foot would probably be the full cost.

There are so many contingencies bearing upon the cost of a house, that it seems to be nonsense to give anything like a general estimate. No two men live alike, dress alike, or make bargains alike; one may be shrewd and careful, the other careless and inattentive; one may spend the money he earns, and which he knows by experience the uttermost value of, and the other may disburse funds that somebody else has earned for him. Then, again, facilities for procuring supplies easily make considerable difference. The well-to-do farmer, located within a reasonable distance of a navigable stream, with stone quarry and sand-bank on his own place, availing himself in the dull season of his own help and teams, and counting all this as nothing— which is the usual style—builds cheaper than the city business man, who hires teams at six to eight dollars a day to haul supplies long distances over hilly roads, and who can not give the time to closely superintend all the details of construction. Contractors will make lower bids in the dull season of the year, and a house put up in favorable weather can be built for less money than when erected in the cold, short days of winter. A mechanic will lay more shingles on a balmy May day than he will

when the searching blasts of January are freezing fingers and
toes.

In the interior finish or trimming of a house, it is the best of
taste to do everything neatly and plainly; elaborate moldings,

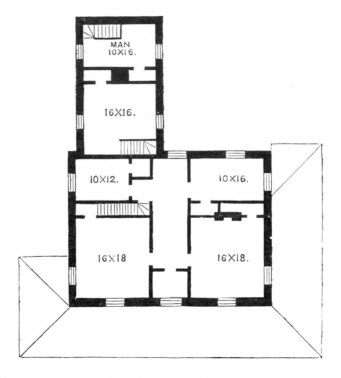

FIG. 69.—SECOND FLOOR.

carvings, panneling, etc., are better indications of wealth than
of taste, and we lean stronger to the side of substantial and sensible expenditure than we do to extravagant show. A style of
finish in keeping with the character of the house and the posi-

tion of the owner is all that should be attempted ; and it would
be better, also, not to make too decided a difference in different
rooms or floors ; not to be too profuse in ornament in the parlor,
and scant and naked in the bedrooms. The work should be
done for the owner's use and enjoyment, and that which is good
enough for him should be good enough for his friends ; better
by far decorate the walls with pictures and the room with meri-
torious works of art, than a trashy display of superfluous wood
and plaster moldings and machine carvings. Beyond their real
useful value, neatly and substantially applied, there is nothing
in interior decoration in wood or plaster that may not be entirely eclipsed by judicious and tasteful articles of real merit, as
thus an air of refinement and comfort will be conveyed that can
not be produced by the rigid stiffness of profuse mechanical
work. One means money ; the other, an inborn and refined
taste which money can not buy.

The surrounding grounds of a country home should receive
careful study, and a well-digested plan would be an economical
and valuable assistant.

No one who wishes a convenient house built with a knowledge of its cost, would go blindly ahead without first preparing
his plan ; but some men like to jump into the dark, while
others look carefully ahead at the landing-place. A plan for the
improvement of grounds has even more combinations than one
for building a house. Its leading features embrace the location
of barn, outbuildings, fruit and vegetable garden, roads, walks,
entrances, lawn, ornamental planting and embellishment with
names and location of trees, etc., all so situated as to be best
adapted for each purpose, and convenient from the house and
from each other. Improvements can thus be carried on year
after year, and harmonize with all the surroundings ; whatever
is done is properly done, and occupies its proper place ; there is
no disposition to change, as no change can be made for the

better; everything can be carried out intelligently and economically, and the best results obtained.

It may be a matter of surprise to many to learn how intimately the arts of design are united with those of construction, or rather the great use made of a draftsman's skill in developing a work of art, exhibiting its effect, and conveying to the most practical mind its most simple form of production. In architecture, machinery, etc., this is admitted, because the general education of popular taste enables us to understand how we can execute an idea on paper, and carry out a practical result in accordance with it; but when we come to a more intricate form of construction, and more particularly that which relates to landscape adornment, we fail, as a general thing, to recognize any principle of design on paper as applicable to the tasteful results we would like to produce. There evidently is a want of knowledge of the manner in which positive results are attainable in the various departments of art. We are too apt to suppose that there is but the one step from conception to execution; that the brain originates and perfects an idea which the same skillful hand at once executes, while in reality we overlook the intermediate links, which, step by step, lead on from the first original thought to the perfect result—a result as finished and thorough in model or plan as in the final execution. Effects, position, color, form, etc., are all studied in advance, individually and collectively, the details arranged, and the impracticabilities discarded.

Perhaps there is no department of art that requires the aid of those principles that facilitate the comprehension and execution of work as that of landscape gardening, nor is there any art to which a system of working drawings is more applicable. As a matter of economy and taste, it is more satisfactory to experiment with a pencil than with real objects; it is better to work out your plan on paper, and then execute with a thorough un-

derstanding of the result. In no other manner can excellence
be reached; we must know effects, beauties, etc., in advance;
and improvements of every class can just as well be studied in
the abstract, and the plans for their execution be as thoroughly
perfected for any form of landscape adornment, as they can be
for any form that is cut from marble or delineated on canvas.
There is an intelligent mode of conveying impressions from
the mind that originates to the hand that constructs; and this
medium between the artist and the mechanic or laboring man
is a well-studied plan, free from all mechanical impracticabilities, and so plain as not to admit of a misunderstanding.

The successful pursuit of Landscape Gardening, like all other
liberal arts, depends upon a thorough understanding of results,
and no work of excellence can be perfected without a close and
careful study, in advance, of all its details and effects. The
assistance derived from the compilation of a design on paper is
of great value, for the reason that one is enabled to secure suggestive beauties, harmonize them, and reject features that are
not desirable, as well as to investigate the practicability or im-
practicability of the mechanical work necessary. How often do
we hear stated, If I were to do this thing again, it should be
managed in another way; that difficulty did not present itself
until the work was nearly done, and it was too late to remedy
it! It did not occur to us that we might have so located that
road, the barn, the garden; in fact, made everything far more
beautiful, infinitely more convenient, and for about one half of
the expense. We see our mistake now, but the deed is done.
What might have been studied out on paper, where all blunders
could easily have been remedied, has been actually executed in
real materials and at a heavy cost.

Intelligent proprietors who seek fine effects with the least
expenditure can readily understand the advantage of studying
plans, for it is a well-known fact, that the arts of design, in

some of their varied applications, afford the power of expressing on paper every stage of progress in the execution of any work of art, and that the whole process of arrangement, its utility, convenience, and harmony, can be traced step by step through all its combinations.

It is quite necessary to adopt some system in carrying forward improvements, so that they shall occupy those places in which they will be of the most value, and that they be constructed in the most advantageous manner. To know what one wants when improvements are undertaken, is to know a great deal; to communicate those wants to others, requires that one should first understand them thoroughly; to understand them thoroughly, it is necessary to study their various developments, from the first conception to the practical working reality, and to do this successfully and economically there is no such medium as a plan.

The two most prominent professional authors of England on this subject, Repton and Loudon, placed the utmost importance on the value of plans, and their great successes were mainly attributable to them. Repton made drawings of everything he devised, and Loudon's published works are profuse in illustrations; his isometrical perspective drawings are evidence of the extent to which he carried, and the value which he placed on, this important accessory to a profession of which he was an acknowledged leader.

EMPIRE STATE GAS MACHINE,

(Levi Stevens' Patents, including Cunningham's Patent,)

For supplying Dwellings, Stores, Factories & Public Buildings.

The Empire State Gas Machine is the most simple and effective means known for producing gas without heat. Its action is automatic, feeding itself with constant supplies of Gasoline, thus securing steady and uniform supplies of gas.

The gas produced is equal to the best known illuminating gas. It is as economical as any other, and is adapted to a wider range of use for lighting, heating and mechanical purposes.

It will maintain its illuminating power under as great a degree of cold as any other.

It is free from danger with ordinary care in using gas.

Its remarkably pure and steady light is pleasant for the eye.

It renders it easy for persons living remote from street gas pipes to enjoy the luxury of a pure gas light, at a comparatively small cost, and with little trouble.

The public are invited to witness its operation at our Store,

620 BROADWAY, N. Y.

Gasoline may be obtained at market prices from the various sources of supply now in operation. Names of reliable parties manufacturing and shipping the article may be obtained on application to us.

No. 1 supplies 5 Argand Burners.
No. 2	"	10	"	"
No. 3	"	20	"	"
No. 4	"	30	"	"
No. 5	"	50	"	"
No. 6	"	75	"	"
No. 7	"	150	"	"
No. 8	'	250	"	"
No. 9	"	500	"	"

MITCHELL, VANCE & CO.,

MANUFACTURERS OF

Chandeliers, Medieval & Architectural Church Fixtures,

ECCLESIASTICAL EMBLEMS,

And every description of Gas Fixtures, Coal Oil Chandeliers and Lamps, in Metal and Glass; with a complete assortment of Lamp Stands and Trimmings, Glass and Paper Shades; also, manufacturers of Gilt and Bronze Clocks.

WAREHOUSE & SALESROOMS,—620 BROADWAY.

MANUFACTORY,—335, 337, 339, 341 & 343 West 24th St., cor. 10th Ave.

NEW YORK.

MINTON'S
ENCAUSTIC

AND

PAVING TILES,

BANKS, CHURCHES,

&c., &c.,

AS LAID BY US IN THE

CAPITOL AT WASHINGTON.

ALSO,

GARNKIRK CHIMNEY TOPS,

AND

PLUMBERS' MATERIALS OF EVERY DESCRIPTION.

FOR SALE BY

MILLER & COATES,

279 PEARL STRET, NEW YORK.

CATALOGUE

OF

ARCHITECTURAL & AGRICULTURAL
BOOKS,

PUBLISHED AND FOR SALE BY

GEO. E. WOODWARD,

191 BROADWAY, NEW YORK.

BOOKS BY MAIL.

All books pre-paid by mail on receipt of the price annexed, which is the lowest retail price.

Books ordered are selected with great care. The best bound copies, and always the latest editions.

All books mailed are securely packed so as to carry safely any distance.

Any book published, not on this list, can be ordered. Prompt attention given to the execution of all orders for the purchase of books, stationery, or miscellaneous articles.

Architectural and Mechanical Books

For sa.e, or sent post-paid on Receipt of Price.

GEO. E. WOODWARD, 191 BROADWAY, NEW YORK.

ARCHITECTURE

ARCHITECTURAL AND MECHANICAL BOOKS.

Riddell's Architect. 22 colored Elevations and 44 Plans........ ...$15 00
Robinson and Tredgold. Carpentry and Joinery. 3 50
Robinson Tredgold and Price. Roofs for Public and Private Buildings 3 50
Ruskin's Seven Lamps of Architecture............................... 1 75
Shumacher's Monumental Designs 10 00
Silloway's Modern Carpentry............... .... 2 00
Sloan's Homestead Architecture 4 50
Sloan's Constructive Architecture...........................10 00
Sloan's City and Suburban Architecture. Large quarto 15 00
Sloan's Model Architect. With Details. 2 quarto vols. 25 00
Smith's Landscape Gardening... .... 1 60
The Interior Decorator and Practice of House Painting.. 2 50
The Grammar of House Planning. London edition. 2 50
Tomlinson's Warming and Ventilation...... .... 1 50
Vaux's Villas and Cottages. Nearly 500 Engravings............. 3 00
Vitruvius, Architecture. Translated by J. Gwilt.................. 3 00
Whildin on the Strength of Materials 2 00

DRAWING AND PAINTING.

Appleton's Encyclopedia of Drawing. (Very full.)............10 00
Binn's Science of Mechanical and Engineering Drawing for Engineers, Architects and Builders................... 4 50
Barnard's Theory and Practice of Landscape Painting in Water Colors.......... .... 8 00
Chapman's American Drawing-Book... .... 4 50
Clark's Elements of Drawing 1 00
Davies. Shades, Shadows and Linear Perspective........ 3 75
Hand-Book of Oil Painting............ ... . 2 00
Jarves. The Art Idea, including an Account of American Architecture, Sculpture and Painting..................... 2 00
Jarves. Art Hints, Architecture, Sculpture and Painting, 1 25
Johnston's Complete Course of Mechanical, Engineering and Architectural Drawing.............................10 00
Knight's Gems, or Device Book 10 00
Knight's Ornamental Alphabets........................... 1 00
Mahan's Industrial Drawing............................. 2 50
McIee's Series of Alphabets 2 00
Minifie's Mechanical Drawing 4 00
Prang's Plain and Ornamental Alphabets.................... 2 50
Simm's Treatise on Mathematical Instruments............. 2 00
Smith's Topographical Drawing................................. 2 00
Smith's Manual of Linear Perspective......... .... 2 00
The Progressive Drawing-Book—Landscape, Architecture and Perspective........... .... 9 00
Warren's Geometrical Drawing............................. 1 50
Warren's Manual of Linear Perspective.................. .... 1 00
Warren's Manual of Drafting Instruments...... .... 1 50

ARCHITECTURAL AND MECHANICAL BOOKS.

ENGINEERING, SURVEYING, &c.

Appleton's Dictionary of Mechanics and Engineering. 4,000
Illustrations. 2 vols............ ....
Austin's Treatise on Calcareous and Hydraulic Limes and
Cements.... ....$2 50
Cleveland's Elementary Treatise on Mineralogy and Ge-
ology 4 00
Cresy's Encyclopedia of Engineering. London edition.... ...25 00
Dana's Treatise on Practical Seamanship.......... .... 1 50
Dana's Text-Book of Geology................. .... 2 00
Dana's Manual of Mineralogy................. .... 2 25
Davies' Elements of Surveying.................................. 3 00
Davies' Geometry................. • 2 50
Davies' Algebra......... .... • 2 50
Ennis. The Origin of Stars, their Action and Light....... 2 50
Ewbank's Hydraulics 6 00
Evans' Millwright and Miller's Guide..................... 2 50
Gillespie's Roads and Railroads 2 50
Gillespie's Surveying. Very full and complete........ ... . 4 00
Graham's Chemistry.. 5 50
Haswell's Engineer's Pocket-Book............................ 1 75
Haswell's Mechanic's Tables........... .... 1 25
Haupt on the Construction of Bridges...................... 4 00
Henck's Field-Book for Railroad Engineers. 3 00
Herschel's Outlines of Astronomy.......................... .. 2 50
Knapp's Chemical Technology.... .... 6 00
Mahan's Elementary Course of Civil Engineering........... 4 00
Mitchel's Popular Astronomy.............................. .... 1 75
Overman's Mechanics for the Millwright, Engineer, Ma-
chinist, and Architect. 150 Illustrations..................... 2 00
Pallett. Millwright and Engineer's Guide........ .... 3 50
Scribner's Engineer's Pocket Table-Book 2 00
Scribner's Mechanic's Companion 2 00
Shunk's Railway Curves and Location 1 50
Silversmith's Handbook for Miners................... 3 00
The Book of Knots. 172 Diagrams................... 1 50
Trautwine's Field Practice of Laying Out Railway Curves 2 00
Wallace. Treatise on Modeling, Constructing and Run-
ning Steam Engines......... ... . 5 00
Wood's Plan of Telegraphic Instruction 1 50
Willock's Navigation. The Ocean, River and Shore....... 5 00

Orders executed promptly for Books on any subject.

GEO. E. WOODWARD, Publisher,
191 Broadway, N. Y.

Agricultural and Horticultural Books

For Sale at Publishers' Prices, or Mailed Post-paid.

By GEO. E. WOODWARD, No. 191 BROADWAY.

Orders executed promptly for Books on any subject.

<table>
<tr><td>Allen's American Farm Book</td><td>$1 50</td></tr>
<tr><td>Allen's Domestic Animals</td><td>1 00</td></tr>
<tr><td>Am. Agricultural Annual, 1867. Pa. 50c., clo</td><td>75</td></tr>
<tr><td>Am. Horticultural Annual, 1867. Pa. 50c., clo</td><td>75</td></tr>
<tr><td>Barry's Fruit Garden</td><td>1 70</td></tr>
<tr><td>Bridgeman's Fruit Cultivators' Manual</td><td>1 00</td></tr>
<tr><td>Book of Roses. By Francis Parkman</td><td>3 00</td></tr>
<tr><td>Breck's New Book of Flowers</td><td>1 75</td></tr>
<tr><td>Bridgeman's Florists' Guide</td><td>1 00</td></tr>
<tr><td>Buist's Flower Garden Directory</td><td>1 50</td></tr>
<tr><td>Bulbs. By E. S. Rand</td><td>3 00</td></tr>
<tr><td>Bement's American Poulterers' Companion</td><td>2 00</td></tr>
<tr><td>Bridgeman's American Gardeners' Assistant</td><td>2 50</td></tr>
<tr><td>Brown's Field Book of Manures</td><td>1 50</td></tr>
<tr><td>Buist's Family Kitchen Gardener</td><td>1 00</td></tr>
<tr><td>Burr's Field and Garden Vegetables of America</td><td>5 00</td></tr>
<tr><td>Culture of the Native Grape and Manufacture of American Wines. By George Husmann</td><td>1 50</td></tr>
<tr><td>Cole's American Fruit Book</td><td>75</td></tr>
<tr><td>Cottage Gardeners' Dictionary. English Edition</td><td>3 50</td></tr>
<tr><td>Downing's Fruits and Fruit Trees of America</td><td>3 00</td></tr>
<tr><td>Darlington's American Weeds and Useful Plants</td><td>1 75</td></tr>
<tr><td>Dana's Muck Manual</td><td>1 50</td></tr>
<tr><td>Dadd's Horse Doctor</td><td>1 50</td></tr>
<tr><td>Dadd's Cattle Doctor</td><td>1 50</td></tr>
<tr><td>De Brueil's Vineyard Culture of the Grape</td><td>2 00</td></tr>
<tr><td>Eastwood on Cranberry</td><td>75</td></tr>
<tr><td>Elliot's Western Fruit Growers' Guide</td><td>1 50</td></tr>
<tr><td>Fuller's Grape Culturist</td><td>1 50</td></tr>
<tr><td>Fuller's Small Fruit Culturist</td><td>1 50</td></tr>
<tr><td>Field's Pear Culture</td><td>1 25</td></tr>
<tr><td>Flint on Grasses and Forage Plants</td><td>2 50</td></tr>
<tr><td>Flint on Milch Cows</td><td>2 50</td></tr>
<tr><td>Grape Culture. By W. C. Strong</td><td>3 00</td></tr>
<tr><td>Garden Flowers. By E. S. Rand</td><td>3 00</td></tr>
<tr><td>Garden Vegetables. By Fearing Burr</td><td>2 50</td></tr>
<tr><td>Gray's Manual of Botany</td><td>4 50</td></tr>
<tr><td>Harasthy Grape Culture, Wine and Wine Making</td><td>5 00</td></tr>
<tr><td>Henderson's Gardening for Profit. New</td><td>1 50</td></tr>
<tr><td>Herbert's Hints to Horsekeepers</td><td>1 75</td></tr>
<tr><td>Jacques' Manual of the Farm. Cloth</td><td>1 00</td></tr>
<tr><td>Jacques' Manual of the Garden. Cloth</td><td>1 00</td></tr>
</table>

AGRICULTURAL AND HORTICULTURAL BOOKS.

Jacques' Manual of the Barn-Yard. Cloth $1 00
Jennings on Cattle 2 00
Jennings on Swine and Poultry 2 00
Jennings on the Horse and his Diseases 2 00
Klippart's Land Drainage 1 50
Langstroth on the Honey Bee 2 00
Leavitt's Facts about Peat, for Fuel. New 1 75
My Vineyard at Lake View 1 25
Mead's Grape Culture 3 00
Manual of Agriculture. Emerson & Flint 1 50
Mayhew's Illustrated Horse Doctor 3 50
Mayhew's Illustrated Horse Management 3 50
Miles on Horse's Foot 75
Morrell's American Shepherd 1 75
Nichols' Chemistry of the Farm and the Sea. New 1 25
Onion Culture 25
Our Farm of Four Acres. Paper 30 cents; bound 60
Our Farm of Two Acres 20
Pardee on Strawberry 75
Parlor Gardener 1 00
Peat and its Uses 1 25
Pedder's Land Measurer for Farmers 60
Quinby's Mystery of Bee-keeping 1 50
Quincy on Soiling Cattle 1 25
Rand's Flowers for Parlor and Garden 3 00
Randall's Fine Wool Sheep Husbandry 1 00
Randall's Sheep Husbandry 1 50
Skeleton Leaves and Phantom Bouquets 2 00
Stewart's Stable-Book 2 50
Saunders' Domestic Poultry. Paper, 40c.; cloth 80
Thomas' American Fruit Culturist. New 3 00
Ten Acres Enough 1 50
Todd's Young Farmer's Manual, Vol. I. 2 50
Todd's Young Farmer's Manual, Vol. II. 2 50
Tucker's Annual Register of Rural Affairs 30
Tucker's Rural Affairs. Four bound vols. Each 1 50
Warder's American Pomology—Apples. New 3 00
Warder's Hedges and Evergreens 1 50
Wax Flowers, and How to Make Them 2 00
Waring's Draining for Health and for Profit 1 50
Watson's American Home Garden 2 00
Woodward's Record of Horticulture, 1866 .... 1 00
Youatt on the Horse 1 50
Youatt on the Dog. New edition 4 00

Orders executed for any book published.

GEO. E. WOODWARD, Publisher,
191 Broadway, N. Y.